I AM NOT SICK
I Don't Need Help!

How to Help
Someone with
Mental Illness
Accept
Treatment

10th Anniversary Edition

Xavier Amador, Ph.D.

Vida Press, New York
2010

On the web: www.VidaPress.com & www.LEAPInstitute.org

Amador, Xavier, 1959 -

I AM NOT SICK I DON'T NEED HELP! How to Help
Someone with Mental Illness Accept Treatment. / Xavier
Amador.

10th Anniversary Edition.

ISBN-13: 978-0-9677189-5-8

© 2010 by Vida Press, L.L.C.

for
Enrĩque and Lou-Andréa

Other books by Dr. Xavier Amador:

I'm Right, Your Wrong, Now what?
Break the Impasse and Get What You Need
(Hyperion, 2008)

Break the Bipolar Cycle
(McGraw Hill, 2007)

I'm Not Sick, I Don't Need Help! 2nd *Edition*
(Vida Press, 2007)

Insight and Psychosis, 2nd Edition
Awareness of Illness in Schizophrenia and Related Disorders
(Oxford University Press, 2004)

I am Not Sick, I Don't Need Help!
(Vida Press, 2000)

Being Single in a Couples' World
(Fireside Trade Edition, 1999)

Being Single in a Couples' World
(Free Press, 1998)

When Someone You Love is Depressed:
How to Help Without Losing Yourself
(Fireside, trade edition, 1997)

When Someone You Love is Depressed:
How to Help Without Losing Yourself
(Free Press, 1996)

A portion of the proceeds from the sale of this book are donated to the
National Alliance on Mental Illness

**To contact Dr. Amador and for information
on his books, LEAP trainings, and speaking schedule see**
www.LEAPInstitute.org

Contents

Foreword
by Pete Earley (2nd Edition)

How would you feel Dad, if someone you loved killed himself?

I was rushing my college age son, Mike, to an emergency room when he asked me that question. He was seeing secret messages in bumper stickers and experiencing rapid mood swings. When we reached the hospital, I felt a tremendous sense of relief. *The doctors there would know what to do!*

Four hours later, a doctor finally appeared and after briefly questioning Mike, declared there was nothing he could do to help him. Mike was convinced that he wasn=t sick and he refused to take anti-psychotic medication.

Because the doctor did not believe Mike was an "imminent danger" either to himself or others, my son was turned away even though he was clearly delusional.

During the next forty-eight hours, Mike decompensated. Only another parent can really understand how agonizing it is to stand by and watch your child slip further and further into a mental abyss. I tried, of course, to intervene. I told Mike that his anti-psychotic medicine would help him think more clearly. But he told me there wasn't anything wrong with the way he was thinking. I tried to show him that he was having delusions, but he disagreed. Finally, I begged him to take his pills. "Please, please, just do it for me!" But he wouldn't. "I'm not sick," he kept repeating. After hours and hours of exhausting conversations, I demanded that he take his medication or leave the house. That threat only made the situation worse. Afraid of what might happen to him on the street, I backed down. The next morning, when Mike caught me spiking his breakfast cereal with his medicine, he became enraged.

Forty-eight hours later, Mike was in police custody. He had slipped outside one morning and broken into a house to take a bubble bath because he felt dirty. Luckily, the homeowners were out-of-town. It took six officers to subdue him. Mike was charged with two felony crimes.

Uncertain what to do, I contacted the National Alliance on Mental Illness (NAMI), the nation=s largest, grassroots mental health organization, and a volunteer there urged me to read Dr. Xavier Amador's book, *I Am Not Sick, I Don't Need Help!*

When I did, I was amazed. Just about everything that I had done to help Mike had been wrong. Rather than calming the situation, my actions had driven a wedge between Mike and me. I had not Listened to him, not Empathized with him, certainly not Agreed with him and finally had not formed a Partnership with him. Those are the four guiding principles behind LEAP, an acronym that Dr. Amador has coined to help teach parents and others how to better communicate with their mentally ill loved ones. When I was arguing with Mike, I had felt frustrated and overwhelmed. In Dr. Amador's book, I found a simple to understand blueprint for parents, siblings, children, and friends to follow. While I was reading Dr. Amador's book, I also realized I was not alone. Others had faced the very same situation that I had encountered with Mike.

I discovered that Dr. Amador's advice came from years of experience as a clinical psychologist. His academic and professional credentials were impressive. He had served as a professor of psychiatry at Columbia University, as director of Research at NAMI, and director of psychology at the New York State Psychiatric Institute. He had worked as an NBC News consultant, appeared on countless television news shows, been quoted regularly in the media, and had been called on by the National Institute of Mental Health, Veteran's Administration, and U.S. Justice Department for advice. Dr. Amador also had served as an expert witness in high-profile cases, including the Theodore Kaczynski "Unabomber," trial, the Elizabeth Smart kidnapping, and the Zacarias Moussaoui "Twentieth Hijacker" case.

But it was another tidbit from Dr. Amador's background that really caught my eye. His brother, Enrique, has schizophrenia. This was important to me, because it meant Dr. Amador not only had professional experience, but also a personal stake in his research. One of the reasons why he had developed LEAP was to help him find ways to better understand his own brother.

Eventually, my son was sentenced to two years of probation and during that period, Mike followed the rules. He attended therapy, participated in group sessions and took his medication. But several months after Mike's court imposed sanctions ended, signs of his illness began to resurface. I was stunned when I discovered that Mike had stopped taking his medication. Despite everything that we had gone through, he had, once again, quit taking his pills. My first impulse was to confront him. *How could you do this again? Haven't you learned any-*

thing? But my wife reminded me of Dr. Amador's book. Using LEAP, she was able to work out an agreement that soon had him back on his medication and into treatment.

In this new edition, Dr. Amador updates his groundbreaking book. He explains how "unawareness" of a mental illness is a *symptom* brought on by the disease. It is *not* a choice that an ill person makes. He gives practical advice about how families and doctors can bridge the gap created by the federal Health Insurance Portability and Accountability Act (HIPAA) that frequently prevents loved ones from being informed and involved in treatment. He summarizes state commitment laws, using simple to understand terms to explain the legal complexities. Since releasing his first book, Dr. Amador has delivered more than more than 300 lectures and conducted hundreds of LEAP workshops. He has taken information from those sessions and added it to this edition. These include model scripts that suggest specific phrases to use and NOT to use. Being able to refer to these passages is much like having Dr. Amador in your hip pocket.

The needs of every individual who has a mental illness are unique. But regardless of that person's specific problems, the basics that Dr. Amador teaches help readers improve their communication skills, help develop trust, and help turn combative situations into cooperative ones.

One night while Dr. Amador was autographing books, a man approached him empty handed. He had left his dog-eared copy at home, he explained, but had stood in line anyway because he wanted to shake the hand of the doctor who had, as he put it, "given me my son back."

I feel the same way.

━━

Pete Earley is the author of *Crazy. A Father's Search through America's Mental Health Madness*. He is a former investigative journalist for the *Washington Post* and the author of several *New York Times* best-selling books.

Preface to the 10th Anniversary Edition
Xavier Amador (2010)

Why write a tenth anniversary edition? Was it because, like many people, I like round numbers? I remember my tenth birthday like it was yesterday. I was so proud to turn "10" and I suppose I am proud, or more precisely humbled, that *I Am Not Sick* has turned ten years old. This little book, which started out as a labor of love, continues to grow in its reach to family members, doctors, nurses, therapists, law enforcement officers and policy-makers. To my surprise it has been translated into French, Spanish, Hungarian, Chinese and Japanese (more translations are in the works). As much as I do see the appeal of round numbers, their symmetry and the ease with which they can be memorized, I did not revise this book simply because ten years have passed since the publication of the first edition. I wrote it because ten years of experience and new science have been acquired and many more people are asking for even more information on the nature of the problem of poor insight, anosognosia, treatment options and how they can help someone with mental illness who is convinced there is nothing wrong with them.

For owners of previous editions you might, at first glance, think the book is merely one third longer — there are seven new chapters. But as you read you will discover that previous chapters have all been revised. My goal was to update the research and to be even more practical and detailed in the advice I give on how to engage someone with mental illness who does not understand he or she is ill. You will learn several new LEAP tools — I now call the specific communication techniques users of LEAP employ "LEAP tools" (you will see why when you read the first chapter on LEAP). In addition, in this new edition I report on recent research conducted on LEAP, opportunities for training in LEAP and about new research that points to the importance of insuring persons with schizophrenia, related disorders, and bipolar disorder are involved in treatment and adhering one hundred percent, or as close to that goal as possible, to the medications prescribed. In this new edition I also make the case for why doctors should be assessing insight and diagnosing anosognosia, or poor insight, whenever they assess a patient with schizophrenia, schizoaffective, bipolar or related disorders. Knowing whether the person believes he or she is ill is critical to treatment planning.

It was nearly thirty years ago (in 1981) that I first learned how my natural instinct to confront denial of illness head-on led to disaster. My brother had just come home after his first hospitalization for schizophrenia. The medicine he had been given brought him back to reality I knew, but within a day of his getting home, I found the pills in the garbage can. Naturally, I asked him why he'd thrown them out.

"I'm okay now. I don't need it anymore," he explained.

Since this ran counter to everything he was told in the hospital, I made a point of reminding him. "But the doctor said you're probably going to have to take this medicine for a rest of your life. You *can't* stop taking it!"

"He didn't say that."

"Sure he did! I was at the family meeting, remember?" I countered.

"No. He said I had to take it while I was in the hospital."

"Then why did he give you a supply of medicine to take home?" I argued, trying to prove him wrong.

"That was just in case I got sick again. I'm fine now."

"No. That's not what he said."

"Yes, it is."

"Why are you being so stubborn? You know I'm right!" I said.

"It's my business. Leave me alone."

"When you got sick, it became everyone's business. And besides, I'm worried."

"You don't have to worry about me. I'm fine."

"You're fine now, but you won't be if you don't stay on the medicine."

"That's not what the doctor said!"

"Then let's call him and I'll prove it!"

"I don't want to talk about it! Just leave me alone," he said as he walked away.

With every dose of "reality" I tried to give him, Henry countered with more denials. And with every go-round we both became angrier and angrier.

I thought he was being stubborn and immature. My accusations and threats to prove him wrong made him angry and defensive. My natural instinct to confront his denial was completely ineffective and made things worse. We got caught in a cycle of more confrontation and denials (what I call the *denial dance*), which pushed us farther apart. The end result was always that he walked away angry. And then he would relapse and end up back in the hospital.

In 1989, when I first started doing research on the problem of denial there were fewer than ten studies in the research literature. When the first edition of this book was published, there were more than one hundred. When the 2nd edition was published four years ago there were just over two hundred. Today, there are close to three hundred! The avalanche of new research on the nature of the problem and how we can best help persons who say "I'm not sick, I don't need help!" continues. We have learned a great deal which I will tell you about in the pages ahead.

One final note, over the last ten years I have given several hundred talks and workshops on the problem of denial and the solutions offered in this book (i.e., LEAP). LEAP seminars have been presented all over the United States, in many cities in France, Belgium, Australia, New Zealand, the United Kingdon, Hungary, Portugal, Turkey and Spain.

Because of the demand my colleagues and I started a training and research institute aptly named "LEAP Institute" (see *www. LEAPInstitute.org* for information and free resources). We have learned a lot about what works and what doesn't. Over the past decade I have learned much from our experience with thousands of patients, families and therapists all over the world, and from the new research. These are the reasons, not the number ten, that I felt a new edition was needed. I am very excited about how much more practical and informative this new book is and hope that you will feel the same.

I end here with a quote from my foreword to the first edition: "After my lecture [about the research on poor insight] I was surrounded at the podium for nearly two hours speaking with family members who wanted advice and a greater understanding of why their loved ones refused to accept help. The yearning of these people to learn more and to talk to someone who understood their frustration was enlightening. I was also struck by the realization that the scientific advances with which I was so familiar hadn't yet reached many of the people who would benefit most from what has been learned. That is why I wrote this book."

This realization, that many clinicians and family members had not yet learned of the research related to this problem, is nearly as true today as it was ten years ago. Tens of thousands are now informed, but given the scope of the problem of poor insight, millions more have not yet benefited from the science you will read about the pages ahead. My hope is that this book will finally close that gap between science and practice.

I AM NOT SICK
I Don't Need Help!

Introduction

If you are reading *I Am Not Sick, I Don't Need Help!* it is probably because you have a loved one or are treating a patient with serious mental illness who is in "denial" and, most likely, is not taking the medication he or she needs to prevent a flare-up of the condition and to recover. Or if he is taking it, he is not doing so regularly. You've tried various strategies that haven't worked and you're seeking information about how you can help him or her to get help.

The first part of this book provides information about the nature and scope of the problem you are about to tackle. Some of you may be tempted to skip this section and go directly to the chapters on LEAP (Part II of this book) — a communication strategy designed to win the trust of persons with mental illness who lack insight for the purpose of becoming a "friend" whose advice they will follow (e.g., to accept treatment, supportive housing and other services) — I have no problem with that and encourage you to do so if your situation is urgent. Or, if the situation is even more urgent, you may want to turn directly to Part III where I provide practical guidance about when and how to secure "assisted treatment" (inpatient or outpatient involuntary treatment). In my mind, skipping ahead would be an appropriate use of this book. If you do that, however, I strongly urge you — after things have settled down — to go back and read the three chapters that make up Part I.

The information in Part I is vital for several reasons. First, it will help you to understand what the newest research has shown about the causes of what may seem to you nothing more than pure stubbornness on the part of the person you are trying to help. Too often, people with these disorders feel that we (I am speaking both as a therapist and as a family member) are their enemies. From their perspective we are adversaries and detractors — definitely

1

not allies. Meanwhile, we scratch our heads and wonder why they seem unable or unwilling to accept the help we offer. In this context it is not surprising that the relationship often becomes adversarial. However, once you understand that the mentally ill person's refusal to accept treatment typically results from a brain dysfunction that is beyond his control, you will see why you shouldn't take it personally or blame him for what appears to be deliberate denial.

Countless times following lectures I have given to professional and lay audiences (family members and consumers/patients), someone will come up and tell me that knowledge of the new research has helped to alleviate guilt. Just as often I am told that this information helps to diminish blame and anger directed toward the mentally ill person who is refusing help. If you are feeling angry and blaming the person you are trying to help (both common and natural feelings) you will be much less effective in what you are trying to accomplish, and your task will be an unhappy adversarial endeavor rather than a positive collaboration.

Just as importantly, however, you will learn why it's so important for you to keep trying. The research indicates that the sooner someone receives medication, the better his prognosis, the less frequently he will be hospitalized, and the shorter his hospital stays will be. It's often difficult to maintain your resolve when you are dealing with someone who wants no part of what you are offering, so knowing just how vital treatment is will help you to persevere.

Once you know the nature of the problem and why you so urgently need to address it, you will be better prepared to understand and implement the new approach to dealing with poor insight and treatment refusal described in the second part of the book. The techniques you will learn – LEAP – are not only informed by the research on insight and medication adherence you will already have read about, but are also based on the results of recent *placebo controlled studies* and on my own clinical experience working with patients and families and supervising other therapists.

I can't guarantee that LEAP will definitely eliminate medication (and service) refusal in the person you're trying to help, but I can promise that if you faithfully follow the guidelines I give, they will help lower tension, increase trust and greatly increase the likelihood that the person you are trying to help will follow your advice. And if my previous experience and the published research are any indication, chances are very good that you can make a very positive difference.

During the time you are working on the problem, you may face the difficult dilemma of countless other family members and therapists: whether or not to force medication by using the psychiatric commitment laws in your state. Doing this can sometimes be a vital part of the treatment process, but it is most effective when it is done in a way that ultimately strengthens your alliance with the mentally ill person rather than destroying it. The third part of this book focuses on the question of when to "commit or not commit" someone to hospital or outpatient treatment[1] against his or her will. You will learn not only the nuts and bolts of how to seek commitment to the hospital, but also how to cope with the difficult feelings this kind of intervention raises for everyone involved. My main goal is to show you how to deal with the accusations of betrayal you will likely encounter and the guilt you may feel, and, most importantly, how to use the commitment itself to build trust and a sense of teamwork with the very person you forced into treatment.

Too often inpatient treatment is crisis-driven and, hence, short-sighted. You can, however, build upon the trust and

---

1. Many states now have outpatient commitment laws. In select cases these laws allow family members and clinicians to seek a court order to medicate the mentally ill person against their will without requiring hospitalization.

gains you have achieved after the person is discharged from the hospital, and I'll be providing you with strategies for doing just that.

Finally, Part IV of the book ties it all together. You learn, in a brief chapter, the theoretical and scientific basis of LEAP, about other forms of psychotherapy that have been found to be effective in lowering symptoms and how the research argues strongly for a revision of how we diagnosis schizophrenia, bipolar disorder and related illness. In short, I argue that we must assess and document whether the person has awareness of his or her illness so we can design a treatment plan that makes sense (LEAP or Motivational Interviewing rather than asking them to fill a prescription they are certain they do not need).

In the last chapter, I tell you about Henry's death – more accurately I tell you about his life and his relationships with his girlfriend, friends, case worker and with his younger brother – me. My intention is for you to draw inspiration and motivation from this chapter. LEAP saved our relationship and gave us many years of joy and hope. In this chapter I hope to share with you something about Henry's remarkable selflessness.

The final chapter is a concise summary of all the major interventions described in the book. It is quite literally a LEAP cheat-sheet in that it will help you to easily remember the essential tools to convince someone in "denial" to accept treatment and services and more importantly, to accept your friendship and support.

Finally, I encourage all family members to investigate and become involved with one of the family advocacy groups and consumer organizations I list in the Resources section (e.g., NAMI). There are many reasons to do so, not the least of which is to feel less alone and more supported in your quest to better the life of your mentally ill relative. These organizations will also help you to feel less ashamed and embarrassed about having a mentally ill person in your family. These feelings are unwarranted and will only hinder you in your attempts to help your loved one.

For too many years I was ashamed about my brother, who has schizophrenia. Despite knowing that he suffered from a brain disorder and that I had nothing to feel ashamed about, I avoided such organizations and kept his illness a secret from my colleagues. It was only after talking with people like myself that I was able to stop feeling ashamed. Because of my own experience, I would certainly understand if you don't feel that you are ready to attend any kind of meeting or conference about mental illness. It is ironic and sad that the instinct not to talk about family problems keeps many of us from receiving the support and information we need to solve those problems. However, you can benefit from such organizations even if you still feel hesitant about getting involved. You don't have to attend a single meeting to learn from their websites or request other literature offered by these groups. I have learned much from these organizations and have found great comfort in knowing not only that there are many other families like mine but also that there are forces at work to change mental health laws, fund research, and improve treatments.

For therapists who read this book, I aim to give you hope that you can reach your patients/clients with serious mental illness who don't think they're ill and refuse your help. Whether you are a mental health professional or a family member, this book will help to dispel the despair that sometimes makes you want to turn your head and look the other way. It will give you renewed hope that you can make a big difference.

Part I

The Truth about Denial of Illness

Knowledge is happiness, because to have knowledge -- broad, deep knowledge -- is to know true ends from false, and lofty things from low.

Helen Keller

Whilst part of what we perceive comes through our senses from the object before us, another part (and it may be the larger part) always comes from our own mind.

The fact that the brain is the one immediate bodily condition of the mental operations is indeed so universally admitted nowadays that I need spend no more time in illustrating it, but will simply postulate it and pass on.

William James
The Principles of Psychology,
Volume I, 1890, Foreword

7

1
A Common Problem

"I am not sick! I don't need help!"
Henry Amador, as said to the author.

"My brother is so ill. He's refused to take the medication. We've tried to talk him into it," said April Callahan, sister of Russell Weston, who is charged with having shot two guards at the U.S. Capitol. "He just wouldn't do it," added his mother, Arbah Weston. "What are we going to do with a 41-year-old man? You can't throw him in the car."
AP wire July 26, 1998.

"There was [this] sick person [who] broke into David Letterman's house. That was her illness. She had an aversion to treatment and to admitting that she had a problem."
Anna-Lisa Johanson, as told to the author.

"My mother wanted us to camp out on his land and convince him to get help. As far as he was concerned we had the problem, not him."
David Kaczynski, brother of the confessed "Unabomber" Ted Kaczynski, as told to the author.

"After Jeff's last manic episode I thought he'd finally realized he needed to stay on the medicine. But last week he stopped taking his lithium again. He says he's better now and doesn't need it anymore!"
Julia, as told to the author.

Whether they realize it or not, everyone is aware of the problem, if only from the newspaper headlines: Many people with mental illness are in denial that they are ill and, therefore, refuse treatment. Those of us who are related to such persons reluctantly see ourselves and our loved ones reflected in those headlines. Julia's predicament, which was never the focus of any news story, highlights a problem encountered by millions of U.S. families, and tens of millions more from around the world, whose names never appear in the media. It is, in fact, a far more common scenario than those involving violence and/ or suicide, which are, of course, the ones we read about. But just like the more infamous examples cited above, Julia's loved one does not think he is ill and does not want to take medication. His denial and refusal may not lead to infamy, but they will almost certainly lead to worsening illness, lost opportunities, and ruined relationships with loved ones.

Many people with bipolar disorder and schizophrenia think of their illness as something that comes and goes. For a short time, Jeff acknowledged he had an illness and took the medication prescribed for it. But after things got better, he decided he didn't need to keep taking the lithium. For Jeff, lithium was medicine to treat his mental illness in the same way that antibiotics are medicines for an infection. When the bottle is empty, you are cured. In reality, the better comparison is that lithium is for manic depression what insulin is for diabetes, a chemical that needs to be taken every day to prevent a relapse or even death. Because both bipolar disorder and schizophrenia are so lethal (about 10% to 15% of all suffers die from the illness via suicide), this analogy is particularly apt.

Even though Jeff took his medication only sporadically, he was still a step ahead of the game, because many people with serious mental illness[2] have never acknowledged that they're ill and refuse to take medication even once.

David Kaczynski, the brother of Theodore Kaczynski, the "Unabomber," told me that even though his brother had terrorized the nation for two decades, the Kaczynski family had received countless letters expressing support, understanding, and condolences from people who were related to someone with a serious mental illness. Like David and his mother, they had experienced the helplessness and heartache associated with caring for someone who was in denial about having a mental illness. In fact, I was one of those letter writers. Like the others, I saw my own situation reflected in that of the Kaczynski family. I've just been luckier because my brother Henry, like the overwhelming majority of people with these illnesses, was never violent.

Far more common than the tragedies that make the headlines are those that test the bonds of family and the moral resolve of the therapists who are entrusted with the care of our loved ones. When once again a bottle of medication is found in the trash or stuffed under a mattress, when we are told to mind our own business, that we are the only one who has a problem, when yet another doctor's appointment is missed, we all come one step closer to throwing our hands up in despair. Sometimes, whether or not we walk away, our *loved ones*[3] do. They disappear for hours, days, weeks, and even years. My brother Henry was in the habit of disappearing for days and even hitch-hiking cross

---

2. Many mental disorders can be very serious (e.g., depression, anxiety, personality disorders and others). However, for the sake of brevity, I will use the term "serious mental illnesses" to refer specifically to psychotic illnesses including schizophrenia, schizoaffective disorder, bipolar disorder, and others.

3. Since this book is written for both lay and professional readers who are trying to help someone with a serious mental illness, there are many terms I could use to refer to the person being helped (e.g., patient, consumer, family member, loved one, etc.). To avoid cumbersome language I will mostly use the terms "loved one," "family member," or "relative," from this point forward. Readers who are mental health care providers should substitute "patient," "client," or "consumer" (whatever the preference), for the familial reference.

country. Some make the headlines anonymously when they join the ranks of the homeless or incarcerated. That used to be my biggest fear.

There are approximately six million people in the United States with *serious mental illnesses*, and literally hundreds of millions more worldwide. The results of recent studies indicate unequivocally that about 50% of all people with these disorders don't believe they're ill and refuse to take the medications that have been prescribed for them. That amounts to three million *seriously mentally ill* Americans who don't realize they're ill. You probably already had some idea of how widespread these illnesses are, but did you ever stop and think about how many family members there are? If we count only the parents of these individuals, there are twice that number of family members! Add just one sibling or offspring, and the number becomes truly staggering. Now here's the real headline: More than ten million Americans have a close relative with mental illness who is in denial and refusing treatment.

Most studies find that about one half of the people with serious mental illness don't take their medication. The most common reason is poor insight into illness.

In the past twenty years, there has been an explosion of research on the problem of poor insight. Among the earlier studies during this period was one conducted by my colleagues and I. We studied more than 400 patients with psychotic disorders from all over the United States. This "field trial" was conducted as part of our participation in the revision of the Diagnostic and Statistical Manual of Mental Disorders (DSM) conducted by the American Psychiatric Association. We measured a wide range of symptoms, including insight into various aspects of the illness and treatment. What we hoped to learn was how frequently people with a mental disorder did not realize they were ill. Our results showed that nearly 60% of the patients with schizophrenia, about 25% of those with schizoaffective disorder, and nearly 50% of subjects with manic depression were unaware of being ill. This main finding has been replicated more than one hundred times in the research literature and is so widely accepted in the field nowadays that, as of the year 2000, the standard diagnostic manual used by all mental health professionals in the U.S. states that, "A majority of individuals with schizophrenia have poor insight into the fact that they have a psychotic illness...." Page, 304 (*Diagnostic and Statistical Manual of Mental Disorders, IV-TR*, American Psychiatric Association Press, 2000).

In other words, when the patients enrolled in our study were asked whether they had any mental, psychiatric, or emotional problems, about half answered "no." Usually the "no" was emphatic and followed by sometimes bizarre explanations as to why they were inpatients on a psychiatric ward. Explanations ranged from "because my parents brought me here" to stranger beliefs such as, "I'm just here for a general physical." Whereas the majority of patients with depression and anxiety disorders actively seek treatment because they feel bad and want help, these individuals, by contrast, were unaware of having a serious mental illness. Unlike people with depression and anxiety, they never complained about "symptoms" because they didn't have any. Indeed, their main complaint was usually feeling victimized by their family, friends, and doctors who were pressuring them to accept treatment for an illness they didn't have!

We were surprised to learn that the problems with illness awareness did not stop at denial of a diagnosis. The unawareness we were documenting was severe and pervasive.

In addition, a significant percentage of those we studied were also unaware of the various signs of the illness they "suffered" from, despite the fact that everyone around them could readily recognize the symptoms (e.g., thought disorder, mania, hallucinations, etc.). The pattern of pervasive unawareness of symptoms shown in the figure below was also found in all the other psychotic disorder patients we studied (except those with

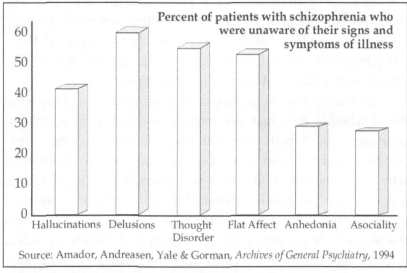

Percent of patients with schizophrenia who were unaware of their signs and symptoms of illness

Source: Amador, Andreasen, Yale & Gorman, *Archives of General Psychiatry*, 1994

psychotic depression). This was the first time anyone had looked at this issue and so we were surprised to learn that the problems with *illness awareness* did not stop at denial of a diagnosis. The unawareness we were documenting was severe and pervasive (i.e., patients were unaware of their diagnosis and unable to see even the most obvious signs and symptoms of their illness).

To illustrate just how extreme the unawareness can be, let's look at Matt, who is a former patient of mine. As you read Matt's story, however, I want you to keep in mind that, in the chapters that follow, you'll also be learning how I was able to help him develop insight into how medication could help him, even though he did not believe he had a mental illness! Not surprisingly, as he was able to do that, the endless stream of conflicts with his family over his refusal to stay in treatment also came to an end.

Matt

At the time I met him, Matt was 26 years old, single, and living with his parents. He had been diagnosed with schizoaffective disorder six years before, when he first began to experience grandiose and paranoid delusions (thinking he was a special messenger from God and knew the President of the U.S.A. personally, and worrying that the CIA was trying to kill him). He had disorganized speech and bizarre behaviors (wearing broken earphones that had been wrapped in aluminum foil). He was hearing voices. Although Matt was remarkably unconcerned about his obvious signs of mental illness, they gravely troubled his family, friends, and even his neighbors, who had to endure his loud speeches. He had been hospitalized on four occasions since he first became ill.

At the time of the interview you are about to read, Matt had voluntarily signed himself into the Schizophrenia Research Ward at Columbia University in New York City, where I was the Science Director. He came to us from a city hospital where he had been taken involuntarily and admitted to the psychiatric ward from the emergency room because his mother had called 911. Although the exact length of time is uncertain, Matt had stopped taking his medications at least six weeks before his mother's 911 call. That night, the paranoia that had been brewing for days boiled over. Matt began to scream at his mother, accusing her of interfering with his mission from God, which, he believed, was to be His special messenger to the President. His speech was disorganized. He was hearing voices. For several days he had been frantically writing letters to the President and trying to place phone calls to the White House. More frightening to his mother, however, he was hearing God's voice telling him to lock her in the closet!

By the time he arrived at Columbia, Matt had been receiving medication for one month. When I interviewed him, nearly all of his symptoms, except the delusions, had shown significant improvement. Although he still believed he was God's messenger and that the CIA was trying to kill him, he felt less urgency about these ideas and was less worried about his safety. In fact, despite his obviously poor insight into the illness, he was about to be discharged to his parents' home with a referral to an outpatient treatment program. I started the interview by asking Matt to tell me how he had come to be in the hospital.

"I think it was... I don't know the exact terms. It wasn't identified to me as of yet. I think they brought me here for a general physical. They wanted to know was I drinking, had I been smoking. I told the police that there wasn't any drinking, no smoking. It was just a mild argument we had and I believe that my mother had more seniority over what was going on. So they took me to the clinic to have the doctor make the determination of how well off I am."

Although Matt's speech was somewhat disorganized and a touch idiosyncratic, I caught the gist of what he was trying to tell me and asked, "So, when you were having an argument with your mother someone called the police." He nodded. "Was it your mother?"

"I think so."

"Why did your mother call the police?"

"I don't know. She wanted me to go to the hospital."

"Why did your mother want you to come to the hospital?"

"She said she didn't really want me to go to the hospital in the event that an argument like that took place, because we were discussing my use of the telephone."

"I am a little confused by what you just said." I admitted "Why did she want you to go to a hospital?"

"We were arguing and I think she thought I was sick and needed to be checked out."

"Were you sick?"

"No. We were just arguing."

"So the police took you to the hospital."

"That's right."

"Why did the people at the hospital admit you?"

"They didn't say. A real friendly guy was there. He said, 'Don't worry you're going to be here for a while and I'd like you to get your thoughts together,' and I've been in the hospital ever since."

"Yes. But that was in the emergency room. What kind of a ward did you go to?"

"I went to a psychiatric ward upstairs. They removed me of my clothes and they told me I was going to stay there for a while."

"But why a psychiatric ward?"

"I think that's all they have available now because of the heavy drug and alcohol use. They may not be receiving aid for a general check-up clinic."

"Matt, now I am confused. Are you saying the doctors at the City hospital admitted you to a psychiatric ward for a general physical?"

"That's right," he answered, as if there were nothing unusual or upsetting about his perception of his circumstance.

"So, do you see yourself as someone who didn't need to be in a psychiatric ward?" I paused and then added, "Do you see yourself as someone without psychiatric or emotional problems of any sort?"

"That's right. But they put me through the emotional tests because of the two-party system.[4] They asked me to cooperate. So I've been pretty much cooperating. Some of it is against my will but I can cooperate."

---

4. I believe Matt is referring to the involuntary treatment law in New York at the time which required two physicians to certify (2 PC) that the person is a danger to himself or others as a result of a mental illness and requires hospitalization and evaluation.

"You didn't want to stay. Is that right?"

"Right."

"Why did you stay?"

"I had to because of the judge. He committed me for a month."

"But after the month was up you decided to come here, to the Schizophrenia Research Ward. Yes?"

"Right."

"But you feel there is nothing wrong with you?"

"That's right. My mother wanted me to come, but there's nothing wrong with me."

To say that Matt had poor insight into his illness is an understatement. Nor does it do justice to the strangeness of the beliefs he had about what was happening to him. Matt believed that police officers had restrained him and taken him to the hospital at the request of his mother simply because she had more seniority than he. He also believed that an emergency room physician had admitted him to a psychiatric ward for one month simply to get a "general physical." And what can we make of the blasé attitude he had while describing these terrible injustices? Handcuffed by the police, taken to a hospital and incarcerated against his will for a month and he didn't threaten lawsuits or scream bloody murder? Many patients with these illnesses do exactly that, while others have the remarkable lack of distress that Matt showed.

I should make clear the fact that Matt had an average IQ. This was not an issue of low intelligence. So then, what is going on here? Is it that Matt was embarrassed by his mental illness and didn't want to reveal the truth to me? That's possible, but if such were the case, wouldn't a less bizarre explanation have been more convincing? More important, however, Matt knew that I was quite well aware of all the details related to his hospitalization. I was, after all, the doctor assigned to his care!

As you may already have guessed, Matt was also unaware that the voices he heard were unusual. He accepted them as if they were nothing out of the ordinary and certainly nothing to be concerned about.

Imagine if *you* suddenly started hearing voices when no one was in the room. What would you do? Very likely you would be worried, and if the hallucinations recurred, you would rush to a doctor. That's what most people would do. I know. I have worked in neurological clinics with such people. Sometimes hallucinations are among the first symptoms of a brain tumor. But why do some people worry when they hallucinate and others don't? Is it simply denial? Is it that some people are more able to accept that they have problems while others are too frightened, proud, or stubborn? Or is there some other explanation?

At this level, poor insight is clearly another symptom of the disorder, and has nothing to do with being defensive or stubborn.

In fact, Matt was not in denial. Instead, our research and that of other clinical scientists tells us that Matt had at least one more symptom that had not been helped by the medicine he was given. His bizarre explanations for why he was in a psychiatric hospital (for a general physical and because all the other wards were filled with drug-addicted patients) and his failure to realize that he was ill and could benefit from medicine, were not stemming from denial or pridefulness. Nor did they have anything to do with being defensive or stubborn. Rather, his poor insight into having an illness and into the benefits of treatment was clearly *another symptom of the disorder itself.* Indeed, the research you will read about in Chapter 3 explains that this type of poor insight is more readily understood as one of the *neurocognitive deficits,* or symptoms of a brain dysfunction, that are commonly caused by these disorders. This is very important information because only when you understand the causes of poor insight can you be effective at dealing with the refusal to take medication that it creates.

2
Staying in the Game

"Far better is it to dare mighty things, to win glorious triumphs, even though checkered by failure, than to take up ranks with those poor spirits who neither enjoy much nor suffer much, for they live in that grey twilight that knows neither victory nor defeat."
Theodore Roosevelt

I wouldn't blame you if you were sometimes tempted to let the problem slide. Whether you are family, friend, or therapist, eventually you get tired of being told, "There's nothing wrong with me, I don't need help." Often we feel so helpless.

Certainly when a mentally ill family member is stable and things are generally going well, it's easy to ignore the problems of poor insight and medication adherence. During those times, we're tempted to sit back and wait for the next crisis to force the issue, or to hope (our own form of denial) that the disease really has gone away. It's always much easier to pretend the situation is not as bad as it appears, because facing the reality of the illness can feel intimidating and hopeless.

Even if we know a mentally ill family member has stopped taking her medication, if things are calm we can't help wanting to back off a little. This is especially true when faced with personal accusations. For example, Vicky, a forty-five-year-old mother of two with manic depression told her worried husband, "I'm not sick anymore. I am not the one with the problem; you're the one with the problem! Get off my back and stop trying to control me!" And if we suspect but don't know for sure that a loved one has been throwing out medications, we often back off because we don't want a negative confrontation to weaken whatever trust we've managed to build up. Later, I will explain that you don't have to back off and what you can do to build the kind of trust that will allow you to persuade a loved one to stay in treatment. But first I need to address the myth that in cases of serious mental illness it is sometimes better to "let sleeping dogs lie."

As Russell Weston's mother remarked in an interview after her son shot and killed two U.S. Capitol Police Officers, "What are we going to do with a 41-year-old man? You can't throw him in the car" and drive him to the doctor. I wouldn't be surprised if, after the fact, she and her husband wished they had at least tried to do exactly that, or that they'd committed their son to a hospital without his consent. But these things are much easier said than done. In Part III of this book, you will learn about forced treatment (aka assisted treatment). Still, the decision to commit someone is very personal, much like your choice to read this book and learn how to deal with denial and refusal to accept treatment. To attack the problem, you must have hope that your efforts will make a difference. Without that element of hope, it's much easier just to let events unfold as they may. Who hasn't thought that, sooner or later, another hospitalization would end the current crisis. And, when there is no crisis, the temptation to "let sleeping dogs lie" is even greater.

Why We Can't Let Sleeping Dogs Lie

It has always been obvious that consistent supervision and treatment help to prevent suicide, violence, homelessness, and reckless behaviors. What had not been clear until recently, however, is the very positive effect that early and consistent treatment has on the course of the illness and the hope of recovery. In addition, recent studies make it clear that focusing on improving particular aspects of insight while ignoring others is vital. Understanding this research will help you to make an informed decision about what to do. If you decide to tackle the problem of poor insight and make facilitating consistent involvement in treatment your goal, the following information will help you to keep your resolve.

||||||||||||||||||||||||||||||||||||||||||||||||||||||||||||||||||||||||||||||||||||||||||||||||||||||||||||||||||||||||||||||||||||||||||||||||||||||||||||||

Research shows that getting seriously mentally ill persons into treatment early, and keeping them there, is very important.

||||||||||||||||||||||||||||||||||||||||||||||||||||||||||||||||||||||||||||||||||||||||||||||||||||||||||||||||||||||||||||||||||||||||||||||||||||||||||||||

According to the new research, whenever someone with serious mental illness has another episode, the long-term prognosis worsens. Some scientists have gone so far as to argue that psychotic episodes[5] are toxic to the brain. The idea is that brain cells are altered or die during and immediately following an episode of psychosis. As yet there is no definitive evidence to corroborate this idea, but there is a good deal of indirect support coming from long-term studies of the seriously mentally ill.

In one landmark study conducted at the Hillside Hospital in Queens, New York, researchers found that those individuals with schizophrenia who received treatment early and consistently had much better outcomes. The results of the study indicate that when antipsychotic drugs are given shortly after the illness first emerges, and subsequent psychotic episodes are treated quickly to shorten their duration, future response to treatment and prognosis is greatly improved.

Similar results were found in a follow-up study involving 276 young, seriously mentally ill persons. The researchers studied these patients during an episode of psychosis and then stayed in contact with them for up to seven-and-one-half years. The subjects who had more psychotic episodes during the early stages of the study did much worse years later. Once again, the results strongly suggest that by limiting the number of full-blown

---

5. [5] Many people refer to psychotic episodes as "nervous breakdowns," but the term nervous breakdown is also sometimes used to indicate conditions other than psychosis. An episode of psychosis specifically involves hallucinations, delusions, and/or extremely disorganized thoughts and behavior.

episodes of psychosis and intervening early whenever the illness does flare up, patients remain higher functioning and less ill later in life.

Finally, in a fifteen-year follow-up study of 82 patients with schizophrenia, researchers found that delays in mental-health treatment and longer periods of psychosis led to a worse prognosis over the long run. This study is especially informative because patients were entered into the research during their very first episode of illness.

The studies just described are but a few examples of the growing body of evidence supporting the efficacy of early intervention for patients with schizophrenia who refuse to take medication. Furthermore, research indicates that the same holds true for other serious mental illnesses including clinical depression with or without psychosis.

In the book *When Someone You Love is Depressed: How to help your loved one without losing yourself,* my co-author, Dr. Laura Rosen, and I review the research on treatment of depression. Most studies find that people with untreated episodes of clinical depression (i.e., those who "ride the depression out") have a much worse course of illness and more frequent bouts of depression later in life.

Other studies show that people with bipolar disorder (manic depression) also do worse when episodes of illness are not treated quickly and effectively. A more thorough description of this important research can be found in the first chapter of *Out of the Shadows: Confronting America's Mental Illness Crisis* by Dr. E. Fuller Torrey. Among the reasons Dr. Torrey cites for getting the seriously mentally ill medical attention are the following statistics:

- About 3 million Americans have untreated severe mental illness
- 150,000 of them are homeless
- 159,000 are incarcerated for crimes committed while unmedicated

Dr. Torrey argues that homelessness, incarceration, episodes of violence, and premature death are not necessary because we know what to do but fail to do it for economic, legal, and ideological reasons. In particular, he cites our hesitation as a society to infringe on the individual rights and freedoms of our fellow citizens as a major obstacle to providing the seriously mentally ill with the medical treatment they need. The issue he takes on is largely beyond the scope of this book, but the case he makes for getting people with serious mental illness into treatment and for finding ways to help them become active participants in their own care is directly relevant. I encourage you to read his book, especially if, by the end of this chapter, you still have doubts about the tremendously positive impact you will have when you help someone with serious mental illness accept treatment.

We must address the twin problems of poor insight and medication refusal if we want our loved one to have the best possible chance of recovery.

What the three studies described above make clear is that when we ignore the problem it not only doesn't go away, it gets worse. We must address the twin problems of poor insight and medication refusal if we want our loved one to have the best possible chance of recovery. In many ways, medication refusal can be seen as a symptom of the underlying problem of poor insight. The good news is that scientists have learned a lot in recent years about the nature and causes of poor insight in serious mental disorders. And the findings themselves suggest specific methods for dealing with the problem. And, unlike some advances in research, this is information you can put to use right now.

Myths and Facts about Insight

The best place to begin is to dispel some of the myths that have been revealed by recent research. One of the most common is that having poor insight is usually a good thing. Many times at clinical conferences a well meaning mental health professional will say, "No wonder he's in denial. If he had insight he might kill himself!" I, too, used to think this way. However, the new research shows that insight is usually a very good thing, but, like most good things, only in moderation. In other words, insight into some aspects of the illness is usually beneficial, while other types of insight can sometimes be detrimental.

Research shows that awareness of the positive effects of medication can be more important to medication adherence than insight into the illness.

In 1991, my colleagues at Columbia University and I published a paper in the National Institute of Mental Health's journal *Schizophrenia Bulletin* in which we proposed several guidelines for researchers interested in studying insight. The first guideline was that insight should be measured in all its complexity. When I use the term "insight" I am referring to much more than whether or not a mentally ill person can say, "Yes, I am ill." There are various things into which one can have insight, and some types of awareness are more vital to recovery than others. For example, a person can have insight into the fact that antipsychotic medication helps him to function in society without necessarily agreeing that he's mentally ill. Research shows that awareness of the positive effects of medication can be more important to medication adherence than insight into illness more generally. I have seen patients who are aware of some of their symptoms while unaware that the voices they alone hear are a sign of illness. Others will say they're ill but don't believe they gain any benefit from taking medication despite objective evidence to the contrary. The guidelines we proposed more than ten years ago are now widely accepted by the scientific community and the pace of research into the problem of poor insight has increased dramatically.

It is also important to recognize that insight is not an all-or-nothing phenomenon; some people have complete insight into every aspect of their illness while others have only a glimmer. For example, Vicky had this to say when I interviewed her in the hospital shortly after her admission to receive treatment for a manic episode.

> *"I am emotionally unstable. I know I lose it sometimes. I get too grandiose and I have to be careful when I get on a roll. But that's just because I am creative."*
>
> *"Is that what your family thinks?"* I asked, knowing that her husband had practically dragged her into the hospital.
>
> *"My family thinks I'm a manic depressive and need to take lithium."*
>
> *"What do you think?"*
>
> *"It's possible that I do, but I don't know."*

Even Matt showed a little bit of insight during the interview excerpted above when he told me, "Sometimes I get really paranoid. It's my nerves."

A glimmer of insight is an open door to developing more.

Regardless of which aspects of insight are being measured, most studies find that the more aware a seriously mentally ill person is of his illness and of the benefits of treatment, the better the prognosis. Patients with better insight have shorter periods in a hospital and have fewer hospitalizations overall. No one knows for sure why this is the case, but it's easy to imagine, especially in light of studies showing that various kinds of insight into illness promote adherence to treatment. In the work conducted at our research center, we found that awareness of the beneficial effects of medication is one of the best predictors of adherence to medication. If you would like more details about these studies, have a look at the recommended books and research literature cited at the back of this book.

Many people believe that side effects – not lack of insight – are the most important reason so many people refuse to take their medication. As it turns out, side-effects play a very small role in treatment refusal while poor insight is the biggest predictor of who will refuse to take medicine. This research finding has been replicated many times over. Side-effects are important, but their role in poor adherence is over-estimated. I believe this has happened because so many people with poor insight give up trying to convince their doctors and loved ones that they are not sick and instead talk about side-effects because they know *that* will be listened to. In a way, they do the reverse of what I will teach you in Part II of this book. Mentally ill persons with poor insight learn to speak the doctor's language and focus on those things the doctors (and, by extension, relatives) want to talk about.

Other forms of treatment adherence are similarly affected by poor insight. For example, Dr. Paul Lysaker and Dr. Morris Bell of Yale University evaluated patients when stabilized and enrolled in an outpatient, work- rehabilitation program. Those with schizophrenia and schizoaffective disorder who lacked insight had very poor adherence to the psychosocial treatments (day hospital programs, occupational therapy, etc.) in which they had agreed to participate, despite a stated desire to work. The researchers concluded that individuals with poor insight are likely to have more problems remaining in a course of treatment regardless of whether it involves drugs or psychotherapy.

Another myth is that the sicker one is, the worse the insight. Actually, most studies find that this is not true. If left unattended, the level of insight is generally stable in most patients. Patients with poor insight while in crisis generally have lower levels of insight even when stable. Whether their symptoms are under control or not, they persist in the belief that they really don't need medication. They may acknowledge that they were sick in the past, but not now. If you are reading this book, it's likely the person you are concerned about fits this category.

I am hopeful that as the scientific community continues to turn its attention to this very serious problem, drug treatments for poor insight will improve.

In a study conducted by Dr. Joseph McEvoy and his colleagues at Duke University, patients with schizophrenia were followed from two-and-a-half to three-and-a-half years after discharge from the hospital. Although symptoms of psychosis improved in nearly all the patients over the course of their hospitalization, those who had been involuntarily committed did not show any improvement in level of insight into the illness. Furthermore, the low level of insight persisted throughout the follow-up period. Not surprisingly, these same patients were more likely to be involuntarily committed over the course of follow-up. The authors concluded that an inability to see oneself as ill seems to be a persistent trait in some patients with schizophrenia, and one that leads to commitment.

I agree with Dr. McEvoy. I have reviewed the literature, and most studies, with only a handful of exceptions, concur. However, this does not mean we should give up hope that medication may help with insight. There is some new evidence, which I will tell you about in Chapter 10, that is promising and bears further investigation. I am hopeful that as the scientific community continues to turn its attention to this very serious problem, drug treatments for poor insight will improve. The last myth proved false by the research concerns the idea that insight into illness when one is seriously mentally ill almost always leads to demoralization, depression, and suicidal thoughts. Suicide is a very serious problem in both depression and schizophrenia. Estimates are that as many as one out of every ten persons with schizophrenia will die from suicide. Like most clinicians, I was taught that poor insight in patients with chronic mental illness, though problematic for treatment adherence, might be a godsend with respect to suicide prevention. The assumption is that patients who don't believe that they're ill are less likely to be depressed and suicidal. Alternatively, those patients who recognize and acknowledge the illness will be more suicidal. In fact, in a study my colleagues and I conducted, we found that, contrary to clinical lore, awareness of having an illness was not associated with increased suicidal thoughts or behavior. This study suggests that poor insight into having an illness is not a protective factor, as previously believed, and argues against the strategy of allowing patients who are unaware of their illness and refuse treatment simply to fend for themselves.

During my graduate training I was also taught that when grandiose delusions (e.g., I am married to someone rich and famous) are successfully treated, the risk of suicide increases. Anna-Lisa's mother (you may recall I mentioned Anna and her mother in Chapter 1) had a delusion that the late night talk show host David Letterman was her husband. When Anna-Lisa's mother committed suicide, it was following a prolonged involuntary hospitalization during which time she was medicated and her symptoms improved somewhat. Her mother's close friends believed that she had committed suicide because the medication had caused her to lose the fantasy world created by her delusions. In other words, when confronted with the reality that she was not the person her illness led her to believe she was, she couldn't bear it. This is a terrible and all too common myth. In reality, it wasn't insight or the loss of her delusions that led Anna-

Lisa's mother to suicide; it was the fact that she did not receive adequate follow-up treatment. She was not working closely with a doctor or therapist she trusted. Had there been someone to help guide her through her new-found grasp on reality, it is unlikely that she would have lost hope and taken her own life. The need for proper follow-up with a trusted mental health professional can't be over-emphasized.

In Summary

The relevant facts revealed by the research are that higher levels of insight into illness predict:

- reliable and consistent adherence to medication
- fewer hospitalizations
- shorter hospital stays
- fewer commitments to the hospital
- active involvement in all aspects of treatment

The research also demonstrates the value of examining the various aspects of insight independently. Having done this, we now know that insight into having an illness generally is far less important than insight into certain early warning signs of the illness and the beneficial effects of treatment. These are the two aspects of insight that the research and my own clinical experience suggest are key to increasing adherence to treatment.

In order to help your loved one increase his awareness of certain symptoms and the positive effects of treatment, you will first need to understand the root of the problem. As you will learn in the next chapter, the research suggests that poor insight in people with serious mental illness usually has little if anything to do with being defensive, stubborn, uneducated, uncooperative or simply difficult.

3

The Root of the Problem: New Research on Anosognosia (Ã-nõ´sog-nõ´sê-ã)

"This is not surprising, since the brain, the same organ we use to think about ourselves and assess our needs, is the same organ that is affected in schizophrenia and bipolar disorder."

E. Fuller Torrey, commenting on the high prevalence of poor insight in persons with serious mental illness.

(*Schizophrenia and Manic Depressive Disorder*, 1996, page 27)

Sitting around the table with me were two nurses, a therapy aid, a social worker, and a psychiatrist. We were in the middle of our weekly clinical team meeting, discussing whether or not we thought Matt was well enough to be discharged from the hospital.

"His symptoms have vastly improved," began Maria, his primary nurse. "The hallucinations have responded to the medication; he's calmer and no longer paranoid."

"Both his mother and father are ready to have him come home again," added Cynthia, Matt's social worker, "and Dr. Remmers has agreed to see him as an outpatient."

"Sounds like we've got all our ducks lined up in a row," the team leader, Dr. Preston, said, capping the discussion and scribbling a note in Matt's medical chart.

"Only one thing troubles me," Cynthia interjected hesitantly. "I don't think he's going to follow through with the treatment plan. He still doesn't think there's anything wrong with him."

"He's taking his medication," I observed.

"For now. But he's really stubborn and so defensive. I don't think that will last more than a week or two after he hits the sidewalk." I had to agree with Cynthia's prediction, but I didn't share her view as to *why* he wouldn't take his medication on the outside.

"What makes you say he's defensive?" I couldn't help asking. Nearly everyone around the table burst out laughing, thinking I was being facetious.

"No, really. I'm serious."

The resident assigned to the case, Dr. Brian Greene, jumped into the discussion. "Well, he doesn't think there's anything wrong with him. As far as Matt's concerned the only reason he's here is because his mother forced him into it. The man is full of pride and just plain stubborn. Don't get me wrong, I like him, but I don't think there's anything else we can do for him as long as he's in denial. No one's going to convince him that he's sick. He's just going to have to learn the lesson the hard way. He'll be back before he knows what hit him."

Dr. Preston, recognizing that Matt's discharge was a forgone conclusion, ended the discussion saying, "You're probably right about that and about the fact that there's nothing more we can offer him here. When he's ready to stop denying his problems, we can help. Until then, our hands are tied. Brian, you're meeting with Matt and his parents at three o'clock to go over the plan. Any questions?" After a moment's silence Matt's medical chart was passed around the table for each of us to sign off on the discharge plan.

"All I need to do is get a job; there's nothing wrong with me."

During the first few years of my brother's illness, before I went to graduate school to become a clinical psychologist, I often thought he was being immature and stubborn. Asked about what his plans were after being discharged from yet another hospitalization, he ritually answered, "All I need to do is get a job; there's nothing wrong with me." His other stock answer was, "I am going to get married." Both desires were natural and understandable, but unrealistic given his recent history, the severity of the illness, and his refusal to accept treatment. Someday perhaps he would realize his desires, but it was very unlikely unless he was actively involved in the treatment recommended by his doctors.

It was exasperating talking to him about why he wasn't taking his medication. Having limited experience with the illness, the only reason for his adamant refusal that I could think of was that he was being stubborn, defensive, and, to be frank, a pain in the rear. I was lucky that I thought of my brother only as being stubborn. Because, like many children of people with serious mental illness, Anna-Lisa often wondered if her mother didn't love her enough to want to get better. It took her mother's suicide to educate Anna-Lisa about what was really happening. And, for myself, it was only after I started working in the field and had met many more people with serious mental illness that I stopped giving such theories much credence. It just never made sense to me that the pervasive unawareness and odd explanations given by people like Matt and my brother could be explained simply as having an immature personality or a lack of love. But you don't have to take my word for it. Let's look at the research for a more objective answer to the question of what causes poor insight and refusal to accept treatment.

Research on the Causes of Poor Insight

I have considered three different causes of poor insight in the seriously mentally ill. It could stem from defensiveness. After all, it makes sense that someone who is seriously ill would be in denial about all the potential and promise for the future that had been taken by the disease. On the other hand, perhaps it's simply the result of cultural or educational differences between the mentally ill person and the people who are trying to help him. Often, differences in subculture and values are blamed. For example, Anna-Lisa always believed that her mother's poor insight wasn't denial so much as a preference for the interesting and fantastic world her illness provided her. When she was symptomatic, the world was a magical place filled with adventures to be had and mysteries to explore. Anna-Lisa never wanted to question her mother's delusions because she feared that by talking about them, she might take them away and somehow cause her mother even more pain. And finally, the third cause I have considered is that poor insight into illness stems from the same brain dysfunction that is responsible for other symptoms of the disorder.

Historically, psychoanalytic theories predominated to explain poor insight in schizophrenia. Although the literature is rich with numerous case studies suggesting that poor insight stems from defensive denial, the question had never been tested in controlled studies until recently.

Everyday defensiveness is not responsible for the gross deficits in insight that are so common in these patients.

Two of my doctoral students, Chrysoula Kasapis and Elizabeth Nelson, took different approaches to this question in their thesis research. Dr. Kasapis examined the overall level of defensiveness in the patients she studied while Dr. Nelson looked at the issue of stigma. Neither approach to the question found anything of significance. Highly defensive patients were generally no more likely to have poor insight than those with little or no defensiveness. Similarly, how stigmatizing patients perceived their symptoms to be had little effect on how much insight they had into their illness. Everyone gets defensive from time to time and some are more prone to denial than others. The same holds true for people with serious mental illness. However, everyday defensiveness is not responsible for the gross deficits in insight that are so common in these patients.

Cultural differences between the examiner and patient may also play a role at times in mislabeling someone as having poor insight. In other words, the patient may be well ware of most if not all aspects of his mental illness, but his sub-culture might label it something else. Consequently, he would not use the label "mental illness" to describe himself. Instead he might say, "I have a nervous problem," or, in the case of religious beliefs such as those common to some Caribbean countries, "I am possessed by evil spirits." The sub-culture of the afflicted person needs to be addressed in any study of insight.

IIIIIIIIIIIIIIIIIIIIIIIIIIIIIIIIIIIIIIIIIIIIIIIIIIIIIIIIIIIIIIIIIIIIIIIIIIIIIIIIIIIIIIIIIIIIIIIIIIIIIIIIIIIIIIIIIIIIIIIIIIIIIIIIIIIIIIIIIIIIIIIIIIIIIIIII

It's ironic, but many patients with poor insight into their own illness are excellent at diagnosing the same illness in others!

IIIIIIIIIIIIIIIIIIIIIIIIIIIIIIIIIIIIIIIIIIIIIIIIIIIIIIIIIIIIIIIIIIIIIIIIIIIIIIIIIIIIIIIIIIIIIIIIIIIIIIIIIIIIIIIIIIIIIIIIIIIIIIIIIIIIIIIIIIIIIIIIIIIIIIIII

Related to the issue of cultural influences is the question of patient education. Has the patient ever been told that he or she has an illness? If so, has he or she been taught how to identify and label symptoms of the disorder? In my experience, most patients with poor insight have been told about the illness they have, yet either claim they haven't been told or, if they recall being told, adamantly disagree, claiming that their knowledge is superior to that of the doctors making the diagnosis. It's ironic, but many patients with poor insight into their own illness are excellent at diagnosing the same illness in others!

The answer to the question of whether half of all people with serious mental illness don't know they are ill because they have no information about the illness is actually obvious when you step back for a moment. If you had heartburn that was bad enough for a friend or relative to convince you to see your family doctor, who then diagnosed the problem as heart disease and explained that the pain was angina, you would stop referring to the pain as heartburn and start calling it angina. You would then make an appointment with a cardiologist and cancel your next appointment with the gastroenterologist. Why, then, do so many people with schizophrenia and bipolar disorder fail to do this? Why do they persist in calling their pain "heartburn" despite all evidence to the contrary?

A Concept of Self that is Stranded in Time

In our paper published in 1991, my colleagues and I proposed that poor insight in people with serious mental disorders is a consequence of, to coin a phrase, a broken brain. We came to believe that pervasive lack insight and the accompanying illogical ideas offered to explain being hospitalized stemmed from neurological deficits. At that time we hadn't yet considered a neurological hypothesis to explain poor insight in bipolar disorder, but we felt there was good reason to believe that what we were seeing in patients with schizophrenia was indeed a consequence of brain dysfunction rather than stubbornness, defensiveness, or ignorance about mental illness in general. The fact is that the brain circuitry responsible for recording and updating self-concept is not working properly in such patients.

My self-concept includes, among other things, the following beliefs about my abilities: I can hold down a job; if I went back to school, I believe I would be a competent student; I believe I have the education and experience to be a therapist, and I am generally socially appropriate when I interact with others. What are some of the beliefs you hold about yourself and your abilities? Do you believe that you can hold down a job? What if I told you that you were wrong, that you were incapable of working and might never find employment unless you swallowed some pills I had for you.

And, by the way, you would have to take those pills for a very long time, possibly for the rest of your life. What would you say to that? Probably the same thing my brother once said to me when I told him he would never hold down a job again unless he took his medication faithfully: "You're out of your mind!" If I said that to you, you would likely think I was joking, and after I convinced you that I was dead serious, you'd come to believe I was crazy. After all, you know you can work; it's an obvious fact to you. If I involved other people, including relatives and doctors, you might start to feel persecuted and frightened. That is exactly the experience of many people with serious mental illness whom I have interviewed. Their neuropsychological deficits have left their concept of self, their beliefs about what they can and cannot do, literally stranded in time. They believe they have all the same abilities and the same prospects they enjoyed prior to the onset of the illness. That's why we hear such unrealistic plans for the future from our loved ones.

If a Man Can Mistake his Wife for a Hat...

If you have never talked to someone who has suffered a stroke, brain tumor, or head injury, what I have just said might seem difficult to believe. If so, I recommend that you read *The Man who Mistook his Wife for a Hat*, by the neurologist Oliver Sacks, who is also the author of the book upon which the movie, "Awakenings" Was based. Dr. Sacks has the gift of being able to describe in vivid detail the inner life of people who have suffered brain damage.

Writing about one case, which became the title of his book, Dr. Sacks describes a man who had cancer in the visual parts of his brain and notes that when he first met Dr. P., a music professor, he couldn't think why he'd been referred to the clinic for an evaluation. He appeared normal. There was nothing unusual about his speech and he displayed a high level of intelligence. However, as the neurological evaluation proceeded, bizarre perceptions emerged. When asked to put his shoes back on, he delayed, gazing at his foot with intense but misplaced concentration. When Dr. Sacks asked if he could help, Dr. P. declined the offer and continued looking around until he finally grabbed his foot and asked, "This is my shoe, no?" When shown where his shoe actually was, he replied, "I thought that was my foot."

There was nothing wrong with Dr. P.'s vision; it was the way his brain was constructing and categorizing his perceptions that was disturbed. Later, when he was sitting with his wife in Dr. Sacks's office, he thought it was time to leave and reached for his hat. But instead of his hat, he grabbed his wife's head and tried to lift it off, to put it on. He had apparently mistaken his wife's head for a hat! When giving talks about poor insight in serious mental disorders I often like to say: If brain damage can cause a man to mistake his wife for a hat, it is easy to imagine how it can cause someone to mistake his *past self* for his *current self*.

In the late 1980s I worked extensively with neurological patients, administering psychological tests designed to uncover the deficits caused by their brain damage. I couldn't help noticing the similarities between the neurological syndrome called *anosognosia* (i.e., unawareness of deficits, symptoms, or signs of illness) and poor insight in persons with serious mental illness. Anosognosia bears a striking resemblance to the type of poor insight we have been discussing. This resemblance includes both symptomatic and neurological similarities. For example, patients with anosognosia will frequently give strange explanations, or what neurologists call *confabulations*, to explain any observations that contradict their belief that they are not ill.

One forty-two-year-old man I evaluated had been in a car accident and suffered a serious head injury that damaged tissue in the right frontal, parietal, and temporal lobes of his brain, leaving him paralyzed on the left side of his body. When I met with him about a week after the accident I asked if he could raise his left arm for me, and he answered "yes." When I asked him to do it, he lay there expressionless, unable to move his paralyzed arm. I pointed out that he had not moved his arm. He disagreed. So I asked him to do it again while looking at his arm. When he saw that he could not move his arm he became flustered. I asked him why he did not move it, and he refused to answer at first. When I pressed him, he said, "I know this is going to sound crazy, but you must have tied it down or something."

Anosognosia has been with us for as long our species has enjoyed the benefits of consciousness. More than 2,000 years ago L.A. Seneca, writing on the moral implications of self-beliefs, described what appears to be a case of anosognosia following hemianopia (blindness caused by brain damage): "*Incredible as it might appear...She does not know that she is blind. Therefore, again and again she asks her guardian to take her elsewhere. She claims that my home is dark.*" How could someone not realize she was blind? And why, when faced with the evidence, would she seek to explain away the blindness?

When one's conception of who one is gets stranded in time, one can't help ignoring or explaining away any evidence that contradicts one's self-concept.

The man who had been paralyzed in the car accident could not understand that he could no longer move the left side of his body. It didn't fit with what he believed about himself (that his arm and leg worked fine), so he couldn't help trying to explain away any evidence to the contrary. He was just like the blind woman who did not understand that she was blind, and more easily believed an alternative explanation (the house was dark) than the truth. Every day someone with a serious mental illness utters similar explanations to buttress his belief that there is nothing wrong with him. When one's conception of who one is gets stranded in time, cut off from important new information, one can't help ignoring or explaining away any evidence that contradicts one's self-concept. And so, many chronically mentally ill persons attribute their hospitalizations to fights with parents, misunderstandings, etc. Like neurological patients with anosognosia, they appear rigid in their unawareness, unable to integrate new information that is contrary to their erroneous beliefs.

One final similarity between neurological patients with anosognosia and the seriously mentally ill involves the patch-like pattern of poor insight. Pockets of unawareness and awareness often coexist side by side. For example, the anosognosia patient may be aware of a memory deficit but unaware of paralysis. Similarly, we have seen many patients with schizophrenia who are aware of particular symptoms while remaining completely unaware of others.

Damage to particular brain areas can result in anosognosia. Studies of anosognosia, therefore, provide a practical starting point for hypothesizing about the brain structures responsible for insight in persons with serious mental disorders. Neurological patients with anosognosia are frequently found to have lesions (i.e. damage of one kind or another) to the frontal lobes of their brain. Interestingly, research has shown that these same areas of the brain are often dysfunctional in people with serious mental illness.

In one study of neurological patients at Hillside Hospital in Queens, New York, conducted in collaboration with Dr. William Barr and Dr. Alexandra Economou, I compared patterns of unawareness in three groups of patients suffering damage to three different regions of the brain. This study was funded by the Stanley Foundation and had as one of its goals identifying the brain dysfunction most likely to produce awareness deficits. As expected, patients with frontal lesions were more likely to show problems with insight into their illness than patients with left posterior damage. Let's look at an example.

George, a seventy-one-year-old man who had suffered a stroke, was asked to draw the clock on the left side of the figure that appears below. Before drawing the clock, he was asked, "Do you think you will have any difficulty copying of this picture?"

George was instructed to use the following 4 point scale to answer the question: 0 = no difficulty, 1 = some difficulty, 2 = much difficulty, and 3 = cannot do. He answered "0" and said he would have no difficulty. The right side of the figure shows the drawing he made after exerting great effort.

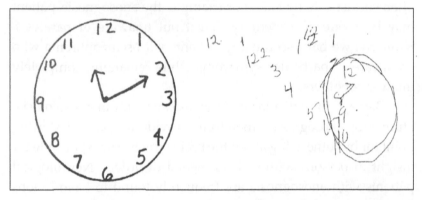

More striking even than his inability to recognize that the stroke had left him unable to perform such a simple task is was happened next. When asked if he'd had any difficulty drawing the clock, he answered, "No, not at all." Further questioning revealed that he could not see or comprehend the differences between his clock and ours. When it was pointed out to him that his numbers drifted past the circle, he became flustered and said, "Wait, that can't be my drawing. What happened to the one I drew? You switched it on me!" This is an example of a confabulation. Confabulations are the product of a brain "reflex" that fills in gaps in our understanding and memory of the world around us. Almost everyone confabulates a little. For example, have you ever heard someone stop in the middle of recounting a something that happened to them and say something like "Wait, I was lying. I don't know why I said that? It didn't happen that way!" This is an example of an instance when someone realizes he has confabulated and corrects himself. Confabulations are constructed memories and/or experiences that are especially common in people with brain dysfunction. However, in such individuals, you don't usually get the self-correction because they don't understand what has just happened. George wasn't lying when he said I had switched the drawing on him. It was the only thing that made any sense to him and so, for a moment, he believed that was what happened.

He was operating under beliefs that were linked to his past self rather than his current self.

In his book *The Principles of Psychology*, William James wrote: "*Whilst part of what we perceive comes through our senses from the object before us, another part (and it may be the larger part) always comes from our own mind.*"

There are few better examples of James's insight than the one I have just given you. George "saw" his drawing using his sense of vision. But his perception of the clock, the image of the drawing that was processed in his brain, was something altogether different from what his eyes saw. George had a concept of himself, a *self-schema*, that included the belief that he could easily copy a simple drawing of a clock. You have the same belief as part of your self-schema. You might not consider yourself artistically endowed, but you believe that you could produce a reasonable facsimile of the drawing if asked to. In a sense, this belief was stranded in George's brain, disconnected from his visual senses and left unmodified by the stroke he had suffered. He was operating under beliefs that were linked to his *past self* rather than his *current self*. He *saw* the numbers drifting outside his lopsided circle, but he *perceived* the numbers to be in their proper place inside a symmetrical circle. Our brains are built to order, and even help construct, our perceptions.

Here is a simple example of what I am talking about. Answer this question: What letter appears in the box you see to the right?

If you answered "E" you saw what the majority of people who are given this task see. But in reality, you did not *see* the letter E. What you saw is a line with two right angles (a box-like version of the letter "C") and a short line that is unconnected to the longer one. Yet, you probably answered E because you *perceived* the letter E. The visual processing and memory circuits of your brain closed the gap between the lines so you could answer the question.

To prove that poor insight in serious mental disorders is neurologically based, however, my colleagues and I needed more than observed similarities with neurological patients. We need testable hypotheses and data that are confirmatory. Knowing that patients with schizophrenia frequently show poor performance on neuropsychological tests of frontal lobe function, we hypothesized that there should be a strong correlation between various aspects of unawareness of illness and performance on these tests of frontal lobe function. Dr. Donald Young and his colleagues in Toronto, Canada, quickly tested and confirmed our hypothesis. They studied patients with schizophrenia to examine whether performance on neuropsychological tests of frontal lobe function predicted the level of insight into illness, and the result showed a strong association between the two. Of particular note is the fact that this correlation was independent of other cognitive functions they tested, including overall IQ. In other words, poor insight was related to dysfunction of the frontal lobes of the brain rather than to a more generalized problem with intellectual functioning. Taken together, these results strongly support the idea that poor insight into illness and resulting treatment refusal stem from a mental defect rather than informed choice.

But just as one swallow does not make a summer, one research finding does not make an indisputable fact. The next step in determining more definitively whether poor insight into illness is a consequence of frontal lobe dysfunction is to replicate the findings of Young and his colleagues in a new group of patients. As it turns out, the finding that poorer insight is highly correlated with frontal lobe dysfunction has been replicated many times by various research groups (see table below). The list of replications I give here will undoubtedly be added to by the time you read these words, as I am aware of yet unpublished results that also confirm the hypothesis. Repeated replications by independent researchers are infrequent in psychiatric research. The fact that various researchers have found essentially the same thing as Young and his colleagues speaks to the strength of the relationship between insight and the frontal lobes of the brain. A few studies have not found this relationship, but in those cases methodological flaws in the design of the research are likely the reason.

Executive (frontal) dysfunction and poor insight
- Young et al. *Schizophrenia Research,* 1993
- Lysaker et al. *Psychiatry,* 1994
- Kasapis et al. *Schizophrenia Research,* 1996
- McEvoy et al. *Schizophrenia Bulletin,* 1996
- Voruganti et al. *Canadian Journal of Psychiatry,* 1997
- Lysaker et al. *Acta Psychiatr Scand,* 1998
- Young et al. *Journal of Nervous and Mental Disease,* 1998

- Bell et al. Chapter in: *Insight & Psychosis*, Amador & David, Eds. 1998
- Morgan et al. *Schizophrenia Research*, 1999a & 1999b
- Smith et al. *Journal of Nervous and Mental Disease*, 1999
- Smith et al. *Schizophrenia Bulletin*, 2000
- Laroi et al. *Psychiatry Research*, 2000
- Bucklet et al. *Comprehensive Psychiatry*, 2001
- Lysaker et al. *Schizophrenia Research*, 2003
- Drake et al. *Schizophrenia Research*, 2003
- Morgan and David (review) in *Insight and Psychosis*, 2nd Edition (Oxford University Press, 2004)

There is also an emerging body of literature linking poor insight in schizophrenia and other psychotic illnesses to functional and structural abnormalities in the brain, usually involving the frontal lobes. A review of these brain-imaging studies (e.g., using MRI, CT and PET scans) can be found in *Insight and Psychosis*, Amador XF and David AS (Editors), Oxford University Press, 2005.

The research discussed above, and other newer studies that link poor insight to structural brain abnormalities, lead us to only one conclusion. In most patients with schizophrenia and related psychotic disorders, deficits in insight and resulting non-adherence to treatment, stem from a broken brain rather than stubbornness or denial.

If you are dealing with a mental health professional who is holding on to the outdated idea that severe and persistent problems with insight are a consequence of "denial" (i.e., a coping mechanism), ask him or her to look at the "Schizophrenia and Related Disorders" section of their *DSM-IV-TR*, page 304:

Associated Features and Disorders
"A majority of individuals with Schizophrenia have poor insight regarding the fact that they have a psychotic illness. Evidence suggests that poor insight is a manifestation of the illness itself rather than a coping strategy... comparable to the lack of awareness of neurological deficits seen in stroke, termed anosognosia.*"*

Now, if the person you are trying to educate is extremely resistant and also a careful reader, he or she may say something like, "Yes, but I also see that Dr. Amador was the co-chair of this section of the *DSM*, so he just wrote what he already believes. It doesn't prove anything!" If that happens, have the person read the introduction to the last revision and he will learn that every sentence in this version of the *DSM* had to be *peer reviewed* before it was added. Peer review in this context involved other experts in the field receiving the proposed text along with all the research articles that supported the changes my co-chair and I wanted to make. *All changes had to be supported by reliable and valid research findings.* So, although the field has been slow to give up outdated theories about poor insight in these disorders (thinking it's denial rather than anosognosia), we are making progress.

New Research on Anosognosia
I have been invited to guest edit a special edition of the National Institute of Mental Health's journal *Schizophrenia Bulletin* focused on Poor Insight in Schizophrenia. This special issue is slated to appear in late 2010. I thought it would be helpful to readers of this book to provide a brief summary of some of the most recent research implicating brain dysfunction as the root cause of unawareness of illness that will be presented in that publication. Below is a brief table listing some of the studies that will be reviewed By Dr. Celine Paillot in that edition of the Bulletin.

Authors	Year	Journal	Results
Young et al.,	1998	*The journal of nervous and mental disease,* 186(1), 44-50.	Lack of illness awareness is related to defective frontal lobe functioning as indexed by neuropsychological measures.
Laroi et al.,	2000	*Psychiatry research,*	
Keshavan et al.,	2004	*Schizophrenia research,* 70, 187-194.	Deficits in insight may be related to a generalized dysfunction of neural networks involved in memory, learning, and executive functions.
Aleman et al.,	2006	*British Journal of Psychiatry,*189, 204-212.	Neuropsychological dysfunction, specifically impairment of set shifting and error monitoring, contributes to poor insight in psychosis
Pia & Tamietto	2006	*European Archives of psychiatry and clinical neuroscience,* 60(5), 31-37.	Lack of insight in schizophrenia may occur as a neurological disease per se following brain damage that seems related to frontal lobe areas
Shad et al.,	2006	*Schizophrenia Research,* 86, 54-70.	Lack of insight is correlated to lower scores on neuropsychological measures that assess executive functions such as The Wisconsin Card Sorting Test (WCST).
Sartory et al.,	2009	*Schizophrenia Bulletin,* 35 suppl.1, 286.	Lack of insight correlated with verbal recognition performance Lack of awareness is best accounted for by poor verbal recognition performance.

Anosognosia versus Denial

Often I am asked the question: "How can I know whether I am dealing with Anosognosia versus Denial?" There are three main things you should look for:

1. The lack of insight is severe and persistent (it lasts for months or years).
2. The beliefs ("I am not sick." "I don't have any symptoms." etc.) are fixed and do not change even after the person is confronted with overwhelming evidence that they are wrong.
3. Illogical explanations, or confabulations, that attempt to explain away the evidence of illness are common.

Ideally, you would also want to know if neuropsychological testing revealed executive dysfunction. But regardless of whether the problem is neurologically based, or stemming from defensiveness, or both, the most important question is: How can you help this person to accept treatment? That is the focus of the rest of this book and the cause of the severe and persistent "denial" may be less important than how you choose to deal with it.

But before we move on to that topic, one last comment about anosognosia will be helpful because many people despair that they will never be able to help their loved one if the denial is in fact a symptom of the illness.

A Broken Brain Is Easier to "Fix"

The bottom line to all of this research is that more likely than not, a broken brain is creating barriers to insight and acceptance of treatment in the mentally ill person you're trying to help. But that is no reason to despair. There are two immediate ways in which you can use this knowledge to benefit your loved one and yourself. First, when faced with the frustration of trying to convince him or her to get help, remember *the enemy is brain dysfunction*, not the person. This shift in your thinking can go a long way toward lowering your level of frustration, increasing your effectiveness, and building a collaborative relationship with the person you are trying to help. Secondly, this knowledge can be used to rekindle hope that you will be able to help your loved one accept the help that's being offered. Hope? If you're like most people, the research I reviewed above may have left you feeling more pessimistic or confused than optimistic! After all, brain damage is irreparable, isn't it? If poor insight is another symptom of brain dysfunction, then what is there to hope for?

A common myth is that personality traits like stubbornness or defensiveness are far easier to fix than deficits caused by brain damage. In fact, however, it is far more difficult to change a person's personality than to teach him how to compensate for some forms of brain dysfunction. So, although the notion that brain dysfunction can cause poor insight may at first lead you to feel powerless, it is actually grounds for renewed hope.

Rehabilitation is possible following many types of brain damage, both because some brain cells can be repaired and more often, because functions can be re-routed to other, undamaged parts of the brain. In such cases doctors carefully assess the deficits caused by the lesions and create a plan to compensate for the loss of ability. This is the usual practice following strokes, brain tumors, head injuries, and other causes of central nervous system damage. In fact, rehabilitation specialists are trained specifically for this task, which is frequently referred to as *cognitive remediation*.

This approach is highly relevant to the task of helping the seriously mentally ill develop awareness of his or her illness and the new skills needed to become willing and active participants in treatment. In the chapters that follow, you will learn how to evaluate the nature and severity of the awareness deficits your loved one has, and to devise a plan for helping him to compensate for these deficits. With this method, you can help him develop the kind of insight he needs (not that he has an illness but instead how certain behaviors lead to positive outcomes) to cope effectively with the illness and accept treatment. Accomplishing this can be much easier than you might think.

Part II

How to Help Using LEAP

"You can't always get what you want.
But if you try sometime,
you just might find,
you get what you need!"

Mick Jagger and Keith Richards
The Rolling Stones, *Let it Bleed*, 1969

4

The Right and Wrong Approach

"Tell me one last thing," said Harry. "Is this real?
Or has this been happening in my head?"
Dumbledore beamed at him..." Of course it is happening in your
head, Harry, but why on earth should that mean it is not real?"
J.K. Rowling, *Harry Potter and the Deathly Hallows*, 2007, page 723

D r. Karen Holloway sighed and said, "Michael's back," as she walked toward where I was sitting in the nurse's station. "I need you to go to the E.R. and do his admission," she added.

"Michael Kass?" I asked, incredulous.

"Afraid so," Karen replied, a bit amused by my surprise. "Get used to it, Xavier. Some patients are stuck in the revolving door, and Michael's one of them."

This was 1988 and Karen was the Chief Resident at the hospital in New York City where I was an intern. To this day she remains one of the more compassionate, bright, and level-headed clinicians with whom I have ever had the pleasure of working. The diagnosis of "Revolving Door Patient" was not one she made lightly or without compassion. Michael Kass had been discharged from the hospital only six weeks earlier after a one-month hospitalization. When he left, he was no longer hearing voices. His delusions still lingered, but he felt little pressure to talk about them, and he was scheduled to receive follow-up treatment in one of our outpatient clinics. Judging by Karen's comment, I guess I didn't hide my disappointment and surprise that he was back so soon.

I took the stairs two at a time, eight floors down, to the Emergency Room—no use waiting for the overburdened elevators—and walked to the door labeled "Psych. E.R." Behind this door, sequestered from the rest of the E.R. service, was a suite of five rooms with four patient bays to the left and the nurses' station to the right. As I entered I took a quick right and ducked into the nurses' station. I didn't want Michael to know I was there until I'd had a chance to talk to the triage nurse. The report I got was frustrating to hear.

After leaving the hospital, Michael went home to live with his parents but never showed up for his first outpatient appointment. His parents, in their late sixties, didn't know that Michael hadn't gone to see his doctor. They'd asked about his appointment, but he didn't want to talk about it. They'd called the clinic, but no one would speak to them about whether or not their thirty-five-year-old son had kept his doctor's appointment. They also didn't know that after the one-week supply of medications he'd been given when he left the hospital ran out, he'd never had the prescription refilled.

I spent about twenty minutes looking at his old chart, which the triage nurse had ordered up from medical records. Then I stepped out of the nurses' station and greeted my new-old patient.

"Hi, Michael, how are you?"

"Dr. Amadorafloor! What are you doing here?" he answered, *clanging*[6], laughing, and talking a mile a minute. "You've got to get me out of here! I was minding my own business—I wasn't hurting anyone—the police got it all wrong. Get me out of here, okay? You've got to get me out because..."

"Michael, Michael, hold on, wait up a minute!" I tried to interrupt.

---

6. [6] A feature of thought disorder, a frequent symptom of psychosis, that involves word associations based on rhyme.

".I'm not supposed to be *beer*. They'll find me here if I stay. Gotta go, gotta get out, okay?"

"Michael, try to slow down and tell me what happened. Okay?"

"I'm telling you what happened. I'm not supposed to be here," he shot back, clearly annoyed with me.

It took almost an hour to get through the checklist I was trained to use. I completed a *mental status exam*[7], evaluated his current symptoms, and listened to his version of what had happened and why he was in the Psych. E.R.. Excusing myself while he was again pleading with me to get him out, I escaped to the nurses' station to write down what I had learned.

Michael was once again hearing the voices of government agents who were commenting on his every move. While we were talking, I asked him what the voices were saying, and he repeated, "He is sitting on the bed, talking with that doctor, he can't escape us now." Given the voices he was hearing, it isn't surprising he'd developed the delusion that some secret federal agency was monitoring his movements and planning to assassinate him.

I noted in his chart the re-emergence of the hallucinations and exacerbation of the longstanding delusion about government agents persecuting him. I also noted that he was not currently suicidal or homicidal, that his "insight into illness" was poor, and a number of other observations I had made while interviewing him. My written recommendation was to restart the antipsychotic medication he'd been on when he was discharged six weeks ago and to admit him to our inpatient psychiatric unit "for stabilization." Then I went back to see Michael, told him my recommendation, and asked him to sign himself into the hospital for a couple of weeks. He refused.

---

7. [7] A cornerstone of psychiatric assessment, the mental status exam involves an assessment of the clarity of consciousness, memory, attention, emotion, thought process, insight into illness, and various symptoms of mental illness.

"The only thing wrong with me is that I'm going to get killed if I stay here any longer!"

Since he had been found hiding in a subway train tunnel and had struggled with the police when they extracted him, I thought we had a fairly good case for an involuntary admission. When he was found, he hadn't eaten or bathed in several days and he had made camp dangerously close to an active track, explaining to police that "they [the federal agents] would never think to look for me here." I called Dr. Holloway; she agreed, and the appropriate papers were signed to admit him against his will for 72 hours. If he didn't want to stay after the 72 hours, and if at that time we felt he was still a danger to himself because of his mental illness, we would take him before a mental health court and try to get a judge to order thirty days of involuntary treatment.

When I explained the plan to Michael, he understandably went ballistic. He was terribly frightened and felt certain that he would be killed if he stayed in the hospital. However, after accepting medication by injection, he calmed down considerably and was moved upstairs to the psychiatric ward.

Unless something was done to engage Michael in treatment, this hospitalization would be nothing more than a band-aid.

Though we had resolved the current crisis, unless something was done to engage Michael in treatment, this hospitalization would be nothing more than a band-aid. He would be "stabilized" and discharged with prescriptions he would never fill and an appointment he would never keep because, as he put it, "I am not sick! I don't need medicine—I need protection from the feds!"

The Wrong Approach

I was using the medical model with Michael, which, in most cases, is the wrong approach to take for dealing with the long-term issue of poor insight and refusal to take medicine. The medical model is supposed to work, more or less, in the following way. Once the diagnosis and treatment are decided upon, the patient is informed of both. If the patient refuses, and if he fits the legal criteria for an involuntary admission to a hospital, the doctors take charge. In some cases, medical doctors operating under a benevolent paternal ethic are able to order treatment against a person's wishes. Like a parent who knows what's best for her child, the physician can take control by admitting the person and treating him against his will. We abide by similar, although less dramatic laws every day (e.g., laws that require seatbelts, mandatory rabies inoculation of pets, and motorcycle helmets; those that prohibit drunk driving, etc.).

My next task under this model was to educate Michael about his illness and the need for treatment. If you are reading this book, you know that when it comes to individuals like Michael, education about their illness does not translate into their gaining insight. And, indeed, that is what happened over the two-week period Michael was in the hospital.

I told him all about delusions and hallucinations and confronted him about his "denial" of the illness. I explained to him the nature of the problems he had and why he should accept the treatment being offered. As he had during his previous hospitalization, once he became more stable, he readily agreed that he would take the medication when he left the hospital. When I confronted him and said, "I think you're just saying that so you can get out of here," he sometimes sheepishly admitted to the lie and told me there was nothing wrong with him except the fact that people wouldn't leave him alone. But most often he would stick to the party line and say, "I know the medication helps me and that I need to take it." Ironically, as some of his symptoms responded to the medication, he got better at consistently feigning allegiance to the doctor's orders.

For people with serious mental illness who are unaware of the illness, this traditional approach rarely works. It rests on the mistaken assumption that the patient has come to see the doctor because he feels he has a problem and wants help. It assumes a collaborative approach from the start: The doctor as an ally, not an adversary.

Although the details might differ, Michael's story of hospitalization followed by outpatient noncompliance, worsening illness, and readmission to the hospital, is all too typical. So was my inadequate response to the bigger problem of what would happen to him when we were done with him (again). I was operating under a medical model that focused on the tasks of diagnosis and treatment. This is the wrong approach when dealing with someone who has, for many years, consistently argued that there is nothing wrong with him and doesn't need help. It's not a bad approach for the short term, but it's mostly worthless over the long term because the "patient" doesn't see himself as a patient.

If you can imagine something like this happening to you, then you have some idea of what it is like for someone with a mental illness to have a delusion and anosognosia.

An analogy might be useful to help you understand why this is so. Imagine I told you that that you did not live where you live. You might laugh and tell me to stop joking around. But what if I produced a restraining order from a court that ordered you to stay away from what you told me was your home address. Now let's say you live with other people, perhaps members of your family, and you saw that they had signed off on this court order. What would you think? And imagine that you then called them to ask why they'd signed off and they said something like, "You seem like a nice person, but if you keep coming around here we are going to call the police. You don't live here, and we don't want to press charges, but we will if you put us in that position. Please stop calling us; you need help!" If you can imagine something like this happening to you, then you have some idea of what it is like for someone with a mental illness to have a delusion and anosognosia.

Stay with the analogy and imagine you went home only to be arrested by the police. The nice people at your address did not want to press charges, so the police took you to the E.R.. Would you be receptive to my advice that you should take psychiatric drugs for your "delusion" that you live where *you know* you live? I doubt it. I have done this role play countless times and the answer is always "No!" When I ask why, my role play partner usually laughs and says, "Because it's the truth. I know who I am and where I live!" Well, that's what its like for a person with a serious mental illness to have a delusion and anosognosia. The medical model is not going to win this person's trust and cooperation over the long haul. Like you or me, if we were in this situation, once the person is out of the hospital and on his own he will not take medicine. If you can see the situation from that person's perspective, its common sense really.

The Right Approach

In my experience, it is often easy to change such an adversarial relationship into an alliance and long term engagement in treatment. It takes some focused effort, but it's not hard to do once you learn the main lessons. The hardest part is putting aside your preconceptions and remembering that no amount of arguing has previously changed your loved one's opinion about being mentally ill. My best advice to you is to stop trying to convince him he is ill. When you accept your powerlessness to convince him you know the answer to the penultimate question (Is he, or is he not, mentally ill?) you will begin to open doors you didn't even know existed. Remember, if you had truly succeeded in convincing your loved one he has a mental illness you would not be reading this book. The first step, therefore, is to stop arguing and start listening to your loved one in a way that leaves him feeling that his point of view – including his delusional ideas and the belief that he is not sick – is being respected.

The first step, therefore, is to stop arguing and start listening to your loved one in a way that leaves him feeling that his point of view – including his delusional ideas and the belief that he is not sick – is being respected.

Professor Dumbledore's answer to Harry Potter's question quoted at the start of this chapter is exactly right. For all intents and purposes your loved one's experience is very real indeed. He truly is not sick. If you can relate to your loved one in this way, you will be much closer to becoming allies and working together to find the reasons *he* may have to accept treatment – even though he is not sick. You don't have to agree with his reality – the realness of his experience – but you do need to listen to it and genuinely respect it.

My colleagues and I have helped many patients accept treatment for a wide range of problems that they feel have nothing to do with mental illness: e.g., to relieve the stress caused by the conspiracy against them; to help them sleep; to get their families "off their back"; to lower the volume on the voices being transmitted by the CIA, etc..

I don't expect you to immediately embrace this idea. Most people find it counter-intuitive and even a little scary. Others like the concept of stepping back from the debate about whether or not the person is ill but are not sure about how it is going to help. Let me start addressing these concerns by describing my approach and the science behind it.

Motivational Enhancement Therapy and LEAP

Anyone who has dealt with severe denial in a loved knows that it can't be fixed simply by educating the person about the problem he doesn't believe he has. Such attempts are futile because the "patient" doesn't see himself as a patient. And, research shows that confrontation and group "interventions" also rarely work. In fact, contrary to what most people believe, "interventions" often do more harm than good! So what does work?

Motivational Enhancement Therapy (MET) is a science-proved method that helps people in denial accept treatment. It was first developed more than twenty years ago for professionals like me who were working with substance- and alcohol-abusing patients. Unfortunately, despite its proven effectiveness for engaging people with substance abuse problems in treatment, few therapists are trained to use it with patients who have a serious mental illness. This needs to change because there is plenty of research to support using MET with such individuals.

In 2002, the *American Journal of Psychiatry* published a review by Dr. Annette Zygmunt and her colleagues of studies published over a 20-year period that were aimed at improving medication adherence in schizophrenia. The researchers found that "...although interventions and family therapy programs relying on psychoeducation were common in clinical practice, *they were typically ineffective* [with respect to improving adherence to treatment]... *Motivational techniques,* [on the other hand] were common features of *successful programs.*" By "motivational techniques" the authors meant the main elements of MET.

I realized almost immediately that the specific communication skills and strategies we were teaching therapists could be learned by anyone.

Relying on the same evidence base reviewed by Dr. Zygmunt and her colleagues, Dr. Aaron T. Beck (considered by many to be the father of cognitive psychology) and I developed a form of MET we called Medication and Insight Therapy (MAIT) for an inpatient research study to be used with people who have serious mental illness. At the time (mid-1990s), we taught this method only to therapists. But I realized almost immediately that anyone could learn the specific communication skills and strategies we were teaching. I felt it was more a communication style than a complicated therapeutic intervention. I came to believe that you don't need an M.D., M.S.W., or Ph.D. to use the main elements of this therapy effectively. Consequently, I developed a lay-friendly version that can be taught to lay persons and mental health professionals alike.

Listen-Empathize-Agree-Partner (LEAP) method

The result was the Listen-Empathize-Agree-Partner (LEAP) method. Over the past six years, since the publication of the first edition of this book, I have taught LEAP to thousands of people across the country and overseas. Although the focus of my LEAP workshops was to show family members and health providers how to convince someone with serious mental illness to accept treatment, people at every seminar have commented on the usefulness of this method across a range of problems. That has been my experience as well. So whether or not you believe your loved one has anosognosia for mental illness, or simple denial of illness, LEAP can help.

5
Learning to LEAP

When I was five years old I wanted to be Batman. It's true that Superman, Spiderman, and the Hulk were also appealing, but for me they were all a distant second to Batman. It wasn't his mask and ears--which I remember thinking looked goofy--it was that amazing "Bat Utility Belt." I had to have a Batman costume for Halloween—nothing else would do. I still remember how I felt when I strapped on that belt for the first time. I could conquer all evil, set things right and live to tell the tale. I had power to do good.

The best thing about Batman was that he was a regular person. He did not have super powers.It was his tool belt--and that's really all it was--that set him apart from mere mortals. There were many high tech tools in that belt, but my favorite was the grappling hook attached to a dental-floss-thin rope that he used to walk up the sides of buildings. With those tools, there was no wall he could not climb, no obstacle he could not overcome. There was no enemy he could not beat.

I want you to imagine that you, too, have a tool belt. It can be made of any material you like, stylish (Dolce and Gabbana) or purely functional looking (Craftsman). Imagine it is full on the left side with all the tools we use when relying on the medical and psychoeducational approaches (e.g., Making a diagnosis, educating the person about his diagnosis, giving him his prognosis and prescriptions for treatment, reality testing about delusions, etc.). These tools are highly effective when we are dealing with persons who have insight and want our help. They are ideal for persons who identify themselves as patients or consumers.

Now I want you to imagine that your tool belt is empty on the right side. Loops, hooks, and pockets all lay open and ready to receive the tools you will need to help someone accept treatment even thought he does not believe he is ill. I'm going to be providing you with the tools to fill that side of your belt. They will serve you well, but you'll have to practice using them.

The first and most important tool you will put in your belt is the focus of next chapter – the *Reflective Listening Tool*. But you will also learn how to not "buy into delusions" while listening without judgment, how to *delay giving your opinion* when asked potentially deal-breaker questions like "So do you think I'm sick and should take this medicine?" (I will also explain all the reasons you should delay answering such questions and choosing the right time to finally give your opinion); and a tool for *giving your opinion* in a manner that allows your loved one to save face, retain dignity, not feel betrayed and most importantly, stay in the conversation and not walk away.

To make all this happen you have to put your goal of convincing your loved one he is sick high up on a shelf, at least for the time being.

I think you will find that LEAP's effectiveness for dealing with someone in denial or with anosognosia is immediately intuitive. Once you learn the basic principles, it simply makes sense that it will work far better than what you've been doing all along. The core tools are *Listening* (using "reflective" listening), *Empathizing* (strategically--especially about those feelings you've ignored during your previous arguments about your loved one's being sick and needing treatment), *Agreeing* (on those things you can agree on and agreeing to disagree about the others), and ultimately *Partnering* (forming a partnership to achieve the goals you share).

More often than not the first aim of LEAP is to repair the damage done to the relationship by your (or other's) previously adhering to the medical model and taking the "Dr. knows best approach." The second task is to help your loved one find *his own reasons* to accept treatment. To make all this happen you have to put your goal of convincing your loved one he is sick high up on a shelf, at least for the time being.

Listen with only one goal: to understand the other person's point of view and reflect your understanding back to him

The cornerstone of LEAP is reflective listening. It is also the one feature of the method that immediately turns down the volume on everyone's anger, builds trust, and mends fences. The reason is that you listen with only one goal: to understand the other person's point of view and reflect your understanding back to him. You don't comment on what he just said, point out ways in which you think he's wrong, judge, or react in any way. Sounds easy until the person starts talking about the fact that there's absolutely nothing wrong and he doesn't need treatment!

Listen

Reflective listening is a skill that needs to be cultivated. It doesn't come naturally to most people. To succeed, you will need to learn to really listen and not react to what your loved one feels, wants, and believes. Then, after you think you understand what you were told, you need to reflect back, in your own words, your understanding of what you just heard. The trick is to do this without commenting, disagreeing, or arguing. If you succeed, your loved one's resistance to talking with you about treatment will lessen and you will begin to gain a clear idea of *his* experience of the illness and the treatment he doesn't want. When you know how your loved one experiences the idea of having a mental illness and taking psychiatric drugs, you will have a foothold you can use to start moving forward. But you will also need to know what his hopes and expectations are for the future, whether or not you believe they're realistic. If you can reflect back an accurate understanding of these experiences, hopes, and expectations, your loved one is going to be much more open to talking with you. More important, he is going to be much more open to hearing what you have to say.

Empathize

The second tool for your tool belt involves learning when and how to express empathy. If there were a moral to each technique, the one for empathizing would go something like this: *If you want someone to seriously consider your point of view, be certain he feels you have seriously considered his. Quid pro quo.* That means you must empathize with all the reasons he has for not wanting to accept treatment, even those you think are "crazy." And you especially want to empathize with any feelings connected to delusions (such as fear, anger, or even elation if the delusion is grandiose). But don't worry; empathizing with how a particular delusion makes one feel is not the same as agreeing that the belief is true. This may seem like a minor point, but, as you will learn, the right kind of empathy will make a tremendous difference in how receptive your loved one is to your concerns and opinions.

Agree

Find common ground and stake it out. Knowing that what *you* want for your loved one is something *he does not want* for himself can make it seem as if there is no common ground. You want him to admit he's sick and accept treatment. He doesn't think he's sick, so why in the world would he take medicine for an illness he doesn't have? To avoid coming to an impasse at this point, you need to look closer for common ground and for whatever motivation the other person has to change. Common ground always exists, even between the most extreme opposing positions.

You will now be able to present the idea that
Medication might help him to achieve his goals.

The emphasis here is on acknowledging that your loved one has personal choice and responsibility for the decisions he makes about his life. When you use the *agreement tool*, you become a neutral observer, pointing out the various things you do agree upon. If invited, you can also point out the positive and negative consequences of decisions your loved one has made. That means refraining from saying things like, "See, if you had taken your medication, you wouldn't have ended up in the hospital." Your focus is on *making observations together*--identifying facts upon which you can ultimately agree. Rather than making an observation or statement about what happened, you ask a lot of questions, such as, "So what happened after you decided to stop taking your medication?" "Did the voices quiet down after you stopped?" "After you stopped taking the medication, how long was it before you went to the hospital?" If you have been using reflective listening and empathy, your loved one is going to feel that you are an ally rather than an adversary, and getting answers to such questions will be a lot easier than it may sound. When you put aside your agenda for the time being you can find a great deal of common ground. For example, if the answer to the question about what happened after the medicine was stopped was "I had more energy but also I couldn't sleep and got scared." You can agree with that observation without linking it to having a mental illness.

At this point in the process you will know the motivations your loved one has to accept treatment (e.g., "sleep better", "feel less scared", "get a job", "stay out of the hospital", "stop people from bothering me about being ill", etc.) that may have nothing to do with the belief he or she has a mental illness. You will know what his short and long term goals are because you will have talked about them together. And with this knowledge you will now be able to present the idea that medication might help him to achieve *his* goals. And again—I can't emphasize this enough—your suggestions may have nothing to do with the notion that your loved one has a mental illness.

Partner

Forming a partnership to achieve *shared* goals is the last and, in my experience, the most satisfying tool you will use. Once you know the areas where you can agree (e.g., staying out of the hospital, getting a job, going back to school, getting an apartment, etc.) you can now collaborate on accomplishing those goals. Unlike the previous techniques, this one involves both your and your loved one's making an explicit decision to work together and become teammates striving for the same goal. You may call the prize "recovery from illness" while your loved one calls it "getting a job," but the names are irrelevant to arriving at a shared plan of action that will, more often than not, involve accepting treatment and services.

6
Listen

In my LEAP seminars I always ask, "Why would anyone want to listen to you if he felt you had not first listened to him? Quid pro quo."This important psychological principle--which is the cornerstone of my method for breaking an impasse--is far from new.More than 2,000 years ago the Roman poet Publilius Syrus said, "We are interested in others when they are interested in us." Psychologists who are expert in conflict resolution and marriage and family therapy have written about this fundamental principle for decades. Dale Carnegie, author of the 70-year-old best seller *How to Win Friends and Influence People* writes, APhilosophers have been speculating on the rules of human relations for thousands of years, and out of all that speculation, there has evolved only one important precept. It is not new. It is as old as history. Zoroaster taught it to his followers in Persia twenty-five hundred years ago. Confucius preached it in China twenty-four centuries ago. Jesus taught it among the stony hills of Judea nineteen centuries ago. Jesus summed it up in one thought--probably the most important rule in the world: "Do unto others as you would have others do unto you".

More recently the authors of *Getting to Yes, The 7 Habits of Highly Effective People, Good to Great, How to Argue and Win Every Time* and other insightful observers of human relations have all emphasized this same fundamental principal of persuasion. But despite the ancient lineage and popular dissemination of this simple and logical truth, it is too often overlooked when we are lured into an "I'm right, you're wrong" situation and end up thrashing around like a fish caught on the end of a line, certain that if we try just hard enough (speak more loudly or repeat our position once again) we will win. And sometimes we do succeed in bending the other person to our will, but not without doing some damage. Listening with genuine curiosity and respect is the key to not getting stuck in this trap and opening the other person to caring about your opinion.

It was 7:30 a.m. and morning rounds had begun on the ward where I worked as an attending psychologist. The entire day shift was seated in a circle around the room. Doctors, nurses, social workers, and assorted students were currently, or soon would be, repeating this ritual on inpatient psychiatric wards all over the country.

The chief of the unit, a psychiatrist, called the meeting to order and then Marie, the head nurse, took over. She began by reviewing how each patient had fared the night before. When she came to Samantha, a forty-year-old, single woman with chronic schizophrenia, she paused and sighed before beginning, "Samantha Green, stable on 6 milligrams of Risperidal, she slept well last night and is ready for discharge today. Jo Anna, do you want to fill everyone in on the discharge plan?" she asked the senior social worker.

"Sure. It's a real gem." Jo Anna answered sarcastically. "Samantha is going back to her parents' house and has an outpatient appointment with her doctor set for a week from today. Mr. and Mrs. Greene are picking her up at noon and she's walking out the door with a one week supply of medication."

"You don't sound too pleased with the plan," I commented.

"It's nothing personal," she replied, knowing that Samantha and her parents also had an appointment with me for a family meeting. "The plan is alright, its Samantha I'm not pleased with!" She paused, and then added, "Look, we all know what's going to happen. Call me cynical, but I'll bet you ten dollars she stops taking her medication before the end of the month and she'll be back here before you know it. She needs long-term hospitalization, not another trip through the revolving door."

Samantha had been admitted to the hospital four times in the past year. Each episode of illness was triggered when she secretly stopped taking her medication. Her parents would notice her talking to herself and start to worry that she was not taking her pills. Her mother would then ask if this was so, and Samantha would invariably deny it even though she had not taken them for weeks. By the time the truth came out, it was usually too late and she needed to be hospitalized.

To my ears, Jo Anna's lack of faith in Samantha, her parents, and in me was neither cynical nor insulting. Given Jo Anna's experience and perspective, she would have been foolish to expect anything more than she did. However, if Jo Anna knew what I knew, she might have shared my optimism for Samantha and her family.

I knew why Samantha didn't want to take psychiatric drugs. It had taken some effort to uncover the true reasons, but with that knowledge and a good idea of what Samantha wanted out of life, I knew I could help her stay on her medication, in treatment, and out of the hospital. But Jo Anna and the rest of the hospital staff hadn't learned what I had because they were focusing on other things.

In the climate of managed care and increasing advances in drug therapies for serious mental illness, mental health professionals working in hospitals have become increasingly specialized. Psychiatrists evaluate health and symptoms and order medications. Psychologists working on inpatient wards typically perform psychological assessments and, less often, do therapy. Nurses dispense medications, monitor patients' health and safety, and provide education about the treatments received. Social workers evaluate the patients' discharge needs and make arrangements for outpatient treatment and residence. As a psychologist working with the seriously mentally ill, I know a good deal about the medications used to treat the disorder but

I don't prescribe them. My job is different. Understanding the person and how the illness has affected his sense of self and goals is one of my areas of focus. And that is why I was optimistic about stopping the revolving door Samantha was stuck inside.

Unlike the others, I knew how Samantha experienced being ill and what she thought about the drugs we were "pushing" on her. I also had a clear understanding of what it was she wanted out of life, and that knowledge had helped me to get her to agree to a trial of the medication as an outpatient. Unlike the other times she'd been hospitalized, she was not agreeing to take the medicine to placate us so she could get out; she was agreeing to continue (for a time) to see if it could help her achieve one of her goals. In other words, I had been doing a lot of listening, and what I had learned gave me a foothold with Samantha and reason to have hope.

Building a Treatment Agreement

The cornerstone of building a treatment agreement that will work and outlast your direct involvement is cut from the quarry of your loved one's sense of who she is, what she believes she is capable of doing, and what she wants out of life. Unless you know its shape, color, texture, and strength, you will be unable to build on this foundation. Each stone you lay will topple and fall to the ground unless you have listened and learned about her experience of these things. Specifically, you want to ask about her:

- beliefs about having a mental illness
- experience and attitudes about medication
- concept of what she can and cannot do
- hopes and expectations for the future

In the next three chapters I will show you how to put your knowledge of these areas to practical use. But before we get there, you have to know your loved one's answers to each of these questions. And because serious mental illness often changes the way people communicate with one another and what each person wants to talk about, there are some common pitfalls you'll need to avoid. The best way to do that is by learning how to use *reflective listening.*

Reflective Listening

We all know how to listen. But I am not talking about everyday listening. I'm talking about *reflective* listening, which is very different.

When you're doing it right, you're asking a lot of questions. You sound like a journalist conducting an interview.

Reflective listening has as its sole purpose understanding what the other person is trying to convey and then communicating your understanding back without commenting or reacting in any way. It is an active, rather than a passive process and your role is purely that of a listener who wants to get it right. When you're doing it right, you're asking a lot of questions. You sound like a journalist conducting an interview. You don't have an axe to grind. I'll give you an example of how and why something that seems so simple doesn't come naturally.

All my life people have told me I am a naturally good listener. As a psychotherapist, I pride myself on my ability to listen and understand other people's experience. But everything I thought I knew about listening was put to the test the first few times I tried to converse with people in denial about having a serious mental illness.

I was 23 years old when I took a job as a "psychiatric

technician" (a.k.a. nursing aid) on an inpatient psychiatric ward at the University of Arizona Medical Center. My brother Henry's first psychotic episode had occurred less than a year before, and despite his rambling speech and crazy ideas, I could still understand him. My experience with my brother had given me a lot of confidence. I had listened to many bizarre things. I could do this.

As a psychiatric technician I was responsible for assessing, among other things, how agitated, depressed, elated, suicidal, or dangerous my patients were. I was also charged with determining whether my patients were following the prescribed treatment plan. Every conversation had a hidden agenda.

My very first admission evaluation was with Barbara, a forty-two-year-old woman who was in the throws of a grandiose delusion and irritable manic episode. She was talking a mile a minute about her power to read minds, her supernatural abilities, the alien implant in her brain that had given her these powers, and the fact that she didn't need to be in the hospital. She was very angry about being there. With a bright-red, hospital-issued clipboard on my knee, I diligently started with the list of questions that were printed neatly in rows on the evaluation form.

"Can you tell me why you came to the hospital?"

"Can you tell me why you came to the hospital?" she mimicked with disdain, effectively making me feel humiliated for being a rookie.

"I am sorry. You were brought here by your husband. That's right, isn't it?" I quickly countered, trying to recover my composure.

"I am sorry. You were brought here by your husband. That's right, isn't it?" she echoed sarcastically.

Stating the obvious, I said, "It sounds like you don't want to talk right now. I am sorry, but I have to get through these questions." I pleaded with her despite the fact that I was feeling even more humiliated and was also starting to get angry.

"I don't give a shit about your f__king questions!"

"I'm sorry, but I really do need to get through these questions."

"Grow up, little boy. You better realize who you're dealing with here. You don't know what you've gotten yourself into and you are in way over your head. Way over your head. Maybe I'll have your head. I could you know. It's as easy as snapping my fingers or blinking an eye or squashing the wings of a butterfly!" she shouted in rapid fire before bursting into hysterical laughter.

My agenda was moot and my face a bright shade of red. I know, because she made a point of telling me as I was excusing myself and trying to walk, not run, out the door. I was scared and angry. I went to the nurses' station and plopped down next to Nancy, the charge nurse.

"You got that done fast," she said incredulously.

"Not really. I didn't get much done at all."

"She wouldn't answer your questions?"

"No. All she did was mimic my every word and threaten me."

"Threaten you?!"

"Not exactly. At least not in reality. She was threatening me with her God-like delusional powers."

"Well, it seems like she may not be able to answer these questions right now. What did you learn about her from just sitting in the room?"

"Well, she's angry and doesn't want to be here. She's in denial. She's manic, irritable, and grandiose. And she doesn't want to talk to me. Maybe someone else should give it a shot?"

"No. She's your patient. I just gave her some medicine . Give her a couple of hours to calm down a little, then try again. Only this time don't bring in the admission form. Start by asking her if there's anything she would like to say. Let her talk about why she thinks she shouldn't be here and see where it goes. Ask her questions about that. That seems to be where she's at. Look for an opening to tell her you're sorry she's here."

"God knows I'm sorry she's here!" I said, joking, and feeling better because I saw the wisdom in Nancy's advice.

I followed her suggestions and ultimately learned quite a bit about Barbara. But it took putting my agenda on the back burner so I could listen to what she was feeling about being forced to be a "mental patient" in a psychiatric hospital. I also was able to get my form filled out. Some questions were not answered, but the essentials were covered. I will tell you more about Barbara later. But for now, I want to focus on the other elements of reflective listening.

To do it right you have to drop your agenda. Your only goals are to understand what your loved one is saying and to convey that understanding.

It's hard to listen reflectively in the face of all the distracting noise ofpsychosis, especially if you are pursuing an agenda and trying to follow a timetable. To do it right you have to drop your agenda, as I did with Barbara. Your only goals are to understand what your loved one is saying and to convey that understanding. This is very hard to do at first, but it's not impossible and actually gets quite easy once you unlearn your natural bad habits. Reflective listening is a skill and, like any skill, once you know the basic principles all you need to do is practice to get it right. To start, here are seven guidelines for reflective listening.

7 Guidelines for Reflective Listening

1. *Make it Safe*
2. *Know Your Fears*
3. *Stop Pushing Your Agenda*
4. *Let it Be*
5. *Respect What You've Heard*
6. *Find Workable Problems*
7. *Write the Headlines*

1. Make it Safe

During the first few years he was ill, Henry never wanted to talk to me about the medicine he was prescribed. He didn't feel safe. As you will learn later on, my brother and I argued a lot, for many years, going round and round on the issue of whether or not he was sick and needed to take medicine. This happened because we got into what I call the *denial dance*, which creates pessimistic expectations about talking. Let me tell you about one of my first experiences with this. My brother had just come home from the hospital and was doing well. The medication obviously helped him. But within a day of his getting home, I found the medicine in the garbage can. Naturally, I asked him why he'd thrown it out. "I'm okay now," he explained. "I don't need it anymore." This ran counter to everything he was told in the hospital, so I made a point of reminding him. "But the doctor said you're probably going to have to be on this medicine for a rest of your life. You *can't* stop taking it!"

"He didn't say that."

"Sure he did! I was at the family meeting, remember?" I countered.

"No. He said I had to take it while I was in the hospital."

"Then why did he give you a bottle of pills to take home?" I argued, trying to prove him wrong.

"That's just in case I get sick again. I'm fine now."

"No. That's not what he said."

"Yes, it is."

"Why are you being so stubborn? You know I'm right!" I said.

"It's my business. Leave me alone."

"When you got sick it became everyone's business. And besides, I'm worried"

"You don't have to worry about me. I'm fine."

"You're fine now, but you won't be if you don't stay on the medicine."

"That's not what the doctor said!"

"Then let's call him and I'll prove it!"

"I don't want to talk about it! Just leave me alone," he said as he walked away.

With every dose of "reality" I tried to give him, Henry countered with more denials. And with every go around, we both became angrier and angrier. I thought he was being stubborn and immature. My accusations and threat to prove him wrong made him even angrier and more defensive. My natural instinct to confront his denial was completely ineffective and only made things worse. We got caught in a cycle of confrontation and denial that pushed us further apart and, not surprisingly, left my brother feeling that it was not safe to talk with me about these issues. The end result of conversations like this was that he walked away. The dance always ends in avoidance.

Henry said it best after one of our early arguments about whether or not he had schizophrenia and needed to take medicine, "Why should I talk about this? You don't care about what I think. You're just going to tell me I'm wrong and need to see a shrink!"

It wasn't until I was in training to become a psychologist that I finally understood that my brother wasn't simply being stubborn. Armed with more knowledge and experience, I reflected on how I had talked to him and realized I had played a big role in getting him to stop talking and start sneaking (e.g., when he secretly threw his medicine in the garbage while claiming he was still taking it). I made him feel unsafe. He knew that if he said he wasn't sick and didn't need medication, I was going to argue with him. Sometimes I did it gently, but as the years wore on and he became what mental health workers call a "frequent flyer," I was often harsh in my confrontation of his denial. Once, I even planned an intervention involving several family members and Henry's social worker. We all, gently but powerfully, told him he was in denial. One by one we told him he had schizophrenia and needed to take psychiatric drugs to get better. Now imagine if that happened to you (assuming you do not have schizophrenia, which was exactly Henry's point of view). Imagine that this conversation followed on the heels of dozens more like it. Would you really be interested in explaining, once again, that there was nothing wrong with you and you didn't need medicine? No. Better to walk away or, if you can't, to shut up and pretend to agree in order to get the conversation over with quickly.

"I am sorry for not listening to you. I understand why you don't want to talk about this anymore."

So how do we make it safe to talk? First, set aside a special time. It can be over a cup of coffee, a walk, on top of a Ferris wheel! Anywhere. What matters is how you introduce the conversation. If you've had arguments in the past, you need to apologize and acknowledge that you made your loved one feel unsafe. You can say something like, "I am sorry for not listening to you. I understand why you don't want to talk about this anymore." And then normalize his reaction to you by saying something like, "If I were in your shoes I would feel the same way." When you apologize for jumping in with your opinion (which I call *reactive* listening) and admit you would feel the same way he does, you make it safe to talk.

But there's more. You have to promise to not do it again. "I want to hear more about why you hate the medicine and I promise I won't do anything but listen and try to get a better understanding of your view on this. I promise not to give my opinion." You might be thinking, "Wait a minute! How can you help someone in denial if you are not going to tell him the truth? Don't you have to help him see the problem and the solution?" Yes, you do. But not yet, and not in the way you think.

Advice is a funny thing. It can be perceived as either welcome or unwelcome, disrespectful, insensitive, and patronizing. What determines how the advice will be received? Here's an example. Women who have been pregnant often complain about how complete strangers walk up to them and give them unsolicited advice. Sometimes it's humorous, usually it's irritating. But almost always, they ignore the free advice because it was uninvited and felt intrusive. And yet, every woman I have talked to about this experience admits that she had at least one friend or relative whose counsel she sought and listened to. That's the difference between *solicited* and *unsolicited* advice. Advice that has been requested carries far more weight than unwelcome advice. So when you promise to not give your advice because your main goal is to listen and learn, you gain instant credibility. And I guarantee, as strange as this may sound, that you will be asked for your opinion far sooner than you would like.

So apologize for not listening well enough, promise you will listen without comment, and keep the promise. To succeed, you will need to discover why you have been afraid to listen in this way, because if you don't, the same fears that kept you from reflective listening in the past will trip you up going forward.

2. Know Your Fears

Whenever I teach reflective listening to a new group of people I am reminded how much more similar than different we are all. On the outside, all sorts of differences jump out at me: the man in the business suit sitting near the one in the "Guns Don't Kill People, People Kill People!" t-shirt and torn jeans; the large, loud woman and the meek, diminutive one. People of all shapes, sizes, religions, races, and politics come to LEAP seminars because they all have a deep desire to help a loved one who is in denial. They also have the same fear about taking that first step. The fear is, "I will make it worse if I listen the way Dr. Amador says I should."

During these seminars I define reflective listening just as I did above. Then I ask for a volunteer. Recently, I did this role-play with Gwen in Halifax, Canada. Her job, as I explained it to her, was simply to listen to me as I role-played a delusional patient, and then reflect back what she had heard. She looked confident as I began the role-play. Speaking fast and sounding very angry and scared, I said, "Look, Gwen, I am not sick, there's nothing wrong with me. I'm not taking that medicine because it will kill me, its poison. If you want to help me, then help me with the people upstairs."

"What about the people upstairs?" she asked without reflecting back what I had just said.

"Every night at eight o'clock they walk across the floor of their apartment to the bathroom. I hear them flush the toilet and I know what they're doing! I'm no fool! They're communicating with the group that's trying to kick me out of my apartment. They're the same people who have been trying to kill me!" Gwen, who had been nodding as I explained the problem answered, "So it sounds like the people upstairs are disturbing you. They're making a lot of noise?"

Seeing that she was done, I asked the audience, "Did Gwen reflect back what I said?" Immediately numerous hands shot up, and, one after the other, they described how she had not. They saw what Gwen could not see in the moment. Although she had responded in the form of a question, as I recommended, she had not reflected back a single thing I had said. The closest she came was mentioning that I was "disturbed" by the people upstairs. In fact, however, I wasn't disturbed, I was scared and angry and it had nothing to do with their being "noisy" neighbors. The noise didn't bother me; it was their use of the toilet as a signaling device that had me upset!

The audience was able to see that she had not reflected back what I had said, but they did not do much better themselves when several of them tried their hand at it. Like Gwen, they omitted mentioning the "crazy" facts. The closest anyone came was acknowledging that the toilet flushing was a signal to the other people in the building who wanted "me" evicted. But they all avoided talking about my denial, my belief that the medicine was poison, and the stranger paranoid delusions (the conspiracy of fellow tenants who were planning my murder).

After reassuring my volunteers that I used to make the same mistakes with my brother before I learned reflective listening, I modeled the correct way to do it. Playing the role of the listener now, I said, "So, Xavier, tell me if I got this right. You're not sick and don't need to take the medicine. What's worse, the medicine is poison. And the thing you want my help with has to do with your neighbors. Every night at eight o'clock your upstairs neighbors walk into their bathroom and flush the toilet to signal other people in the building. These are the same people who have been trying to kick you out and also kill you. Do I have that right?"

Not even halfway through saying this, I could see several people squirming in their seats, shaking their heads, and frowning. "I know that many of you are very uncomfortable with what I just said. What makes you so uneasy?"

"You're reinforcing the denial!" one man practically shouted.

"You can't tell this guy his medicine is poison. He'll never take it!" Gwen added.

"What else worries you?" I asked the group.

"You worsened the delusion; now you're going to get drawn into it. He's going to want you to do something about his neighbors," another man offered. A woman, who I knew to be a social worker, raised her hand and said, "This goes against everything I was taught. You can't collude with a delusion like that. You'll reinforce it!"

"Was anyone feeling okay about what I did?" I asked the group. An elderly woman in the front row raised her hand, slowly stood up, and said, "I thought it was fine. He's going to want to talk with you because you are talking about what's important. He doesn't believe he's crazy and thinks people are trying to kill him, for gosh sake!"

"So why do you think the rest of them are so uncomfortable with my reflecting all that back to him?" I asked.

She slowly turned around to look at the audience, then, turning to face me again, she said simply, "They're chicken," and sat back down. After the laughter subsided I thanked my unexpected accomplice and elaborated on her wise observation.

When you're facing someone who rigidly holds irrational beliefs, you gain nothing by disagreeing.

First, I never agreed with his beliefs about being sick, the medicine, or the paranoid ideas. By prefacing and ending my statements with questions ("Tell me if I got this right." and "Do I have that right?"), I was free to use my patient's own words. In no way did I challenge his beliefs. Why should I? He's delusional! Rather, I showed him, through my actions, that I wanted only to listen to him and understand. I have never talked anyone out of a delusion, and, to my knowledge, I have never talked anyone into one either. The point is, when you're facing someone who rigidly holds irrational beliefs, you gain nothing by disagreeing. More important, you lose that person's willingness to talk about the problem.

There are, however, a few pitfalls you have to watch out for. One is when the person asks, "So it sounds like you agree with me. Do you?" Or the flip side of the same coin: "Why are you acting like you believe me?" Actually, these questions offer an important opportunity, which I'll talk about in the following chapter.For now, I ask that you trust me and for the time being, focus on uncovering what your fears are.

3. Stop Pushing Your Agenda.

I know your agenda is to help someone you're worried about. And you have specific ideas about how the help should come. But because the person in denial is already expecting unwelcome advice for a problem he doesn't believe he has, you need to keep this agenda to yourself!When reflectively listening, the only stated agenda you should have is your desire to listen and learn. When a person trusts that you will not pontificate about what he should and should not be doing, he will be more apt to agree to talk about certain "hot" topics (e.g., his refusal to seek professional help). Agreeing on an agenda is easy if you follow the lead of the person in denial. This is how I was finally able to engage Barbara. What she wanted to talk about was how furious she was for being forced into the hospital when she wasn't mentally ill. If the person you're trying to talk to is upset about having to take medicine, ask him about his *feelings*, not about the medicine or your belief that he should take it. You can say, "I'd like to understand why you hate taking your medicine. Would you mind talking with me about that? I promise I won't pressure you or bug you—I really just want to understand how you feel about it." Try it once with any hot topic and see what happens.

4. Let it Be.

If the discussion turns into an argument and you feel the denial dance coming on, stop! If your loved one becomes accusatory, saying something like, "You don't care about me, all you're thinking about is yourself!" just let it be. Don't fan the flames.

Sometimes mental illness creates "thought disorder," making it especially difficult for others to follow the person's train of thought. It's annoying and frustrating. When talking with someone who has thought disorder, or disorganized speech, be careful that you don't inadvertently impose order on the chaos, because usually you will get it wrong. In other words, let it be and focus on listening *differently* instead of on trying to impose order. Listen for the feelings behind the words and reflect back the emotion. When you understand the underlying emotions, you will discover what the person cares about most and what motivates him.

5. Respect what you've heard.

When you make it a point to communicate your understanding of what you've just heard without reacting to it, you convey your respect for the other person's point of view. You also deflate anger. When you echo what you've heard without comment or criticism, you stop the denial dance dead in its tracks. Think of it this way: Would you really be interested in hearing the opinion of someone you've been arguing with if you felt he or she hadn't listened to your views?

6. Find Workable Problems

Everyone in denial, or with anosognosia, knows he has at least one problem. The problem is you and everyone else who is telling him he needs help! He will have other problems you can uncover as well. Understanding how the person in denial sees himself and his beliefs about what's not working in his life is the key to unlocking the isolation and building a relationship with someone who recognizes he is in trouble and needs help. A relationship with someone who can lead him to that help is the only way he'll find it as long as he is unaware of the illness.

Consequently, you first need to learn what *he* thinks the problem is. How does he define it? And what does he say he needs to fix it? Without understanding what he thinks is wrong and needs to change, you will be powerless. For example, my brother never agreed that he had schizophrenia, but he did think that being forced into a psychiatric hospital again and again was a big problem. I couldn't have agreed with him more. Once you find a problem you can work on together (e.g., Henry and I agreed that avoiding another hospitalization was a good thing), you have common ground and leverage. It is also vital that you find out what he wants out of life, in the short term and in the long term, without being judgmental. You need to find out what it is that is most important to him.

7. Write the Headlines

I started out by telling you that to do this right you need to approach your loved one the way a journalist would. That means not only asking questions without injecting your criticism or other opinions but also discovering a theme and figuring out what the headlines are. So, after a conversation in which you've been reflectively listening, think of the front page of a newspaper and literally write down the headlines. If you can, write them down in front of the person (I will give you examples of how to do this later), so that you know you are both on the same page about what's important to him.

So what are the headlines? The headlines are the problems the mentally ill person believes he has (not the problems you say he has) and the things that motivate him to change (those that are most important to him). Ultimately you are going to work together on the problem as he defines it but link it to the help you believe he needs. And you will do this by harnessing what motivates him.

To illustrate these listening guidelines, I offer the following two examples from families I have worked with. The first is a good example of how *not* to listen while the second provides an excellent lesson on how to do it right. Both examples are drawn from my work supervising therapists in training on an inpatient psychiatric ward. Because my students typically bring video tapes of their sessions with families to our supervision meetings, I can comment on both the therapist and the family members' listening skills.

Ineffective Listening

It was 3 o'clock and Dr. Brian Greene, a second-year resident in psychiatry, was meeting with Matt Blackburn and his parents. Matt is the twenty-six-year-old man who lives at home with his parents about whom I first told you in Chapter 1. As you may recall, he was admitted to the hospital believing he was a close confidant of the U.S. President. He also believed that God had chosen him as his special messenger to world leaders, that the CIA was trying to assassinate him, and that his mother was trying to sabotage his mission (this last belief was not entirely delusional).When he was admitted to the hospital, he also had thought disorder (rambling disconnected thoughts strung together so that when he spoke it was often difficult to make sense of what he was saying) and was hearing voices. After two weeks of treatment at Columbia his speech was more cogent and the voices had quieted down a bit thanks to the medication he had received. He still had the same delusional beliefs, but the drugs helped relieve the pressure he felt to act on them (e.g., go to Washington to meet with the President). The meeting was called by Dr. Greene to discuss what Matt would do after being discharged from the hospital.

"Mr. Blackburn, Mrs. Blackburn," Brian said to each as he shook their hands, "Please come in and have a seat." Matt was already seated at the end of a long table in the patient dining room. His mother circled the table to reach her son and bent down to give him a kiss. Mr. Blackburn immediately sat down in the nearest chair, which was also the farthest from Matt, and started asking questions of Dr. Greene.

"I know we're supposed to be talking about Matt's discharge, but don't you think he needs to stay here longer? I don't think he's ready to come home yet."

"There's really nothing more we can offer him here, Mr. Blackburn," Brian answered. In truth, it probably would have helped Matt to stay another week, but his insurance had run out.

"Well, I don't think he's ready and neither does his mother!"

"Hold on," Mrs. Blackburn said, "I didn't say that exactly. Of course we want you to come home," she said, directing her last comment to Matt. "We're just worried about what's going to happen next."

Seizing the opportunity, Brian began. "Matt has an appointment later this week with a doctor in our outpatient clinic, he has enough medicine with him to last until that appointment, and the hospital Day Program has accepted him. He can start there as soon as the doctor has seen him."

"This is exactly what I was afraid of," Matt's father said to his wife. Then he turned to face Brian and added, "I don't want to be negative, Dr. Greene, but he'll never go to that appointment and he won't go to this day program you're talking about. He doesn't think there's anything wrong with him. We need a better plan than this. Matt won't take his pills and he doesn't like hanging around the people in these programs. He says they're all crazy!"

"Matt, what do you have to say about all this?" Brian rightly asked.

"I said I'd go. I'll go!" he responded loudly while looking down at the table.

"That's what you promised us before, Matt," his father said in a kinder tone. "But when we get home you disappear into your room and you don't go anywhere."

"It's different this time. I'll go! I just want to get out of here and get a job and my own place."

"Are you sure you'll go?" his mother asked, looking worried.

"Yeah, Mom, don't worry, I'll go. I really will. Okay?"

Matt's father didn't look convinced, but his mother and doctor looked, if not convinced, at least relieved by what they had just heard.

Let's review the seven listening guidelines I gave above. Did Dr. Greene and Matt's parents:

1. Make It Safe?

Brian and Matt's family did set aside a special time to talk but did not make the conversation "special" in the way I described above. There was no acknowledgment of their differing views and no apology for previous attempts to convince Matt he was in denial and mentally ill. No one explained that he or she wanted only to hear Matt's views on the discharge plan. And no promise was made to refrain from giving unsolicited advice. Instead, the old argument was immediately raised by his father and the battle lines drawn. The result was that Matt got defensive and then did what you and I would have done had we, like Matt, been through this a hundred times before. He lied and said he would go to the appointment. He lied to get his parents and his doctor off his back and to get released from the hospital.

2. Know Their Fears?

On the surface, Matt's father and mother both appeared to be in touch with the fear they felt going into this conversation. But they were not. They were aware of their fear that their son would continue his career as a frequent flyer, or revolving-door patient. But they had no awareness of the specific fear they had about this conversation, which was that they would make things worse if they did not make their views known once again. Although she did it more gently than her husband, Matt's mother also laid down the battle lines. She wanted her son to stay in the hospital longer. She made it very clear she thought he was still very sick. Both parents, and Dr. Greene for that matter, felt compelled by their fears to once again tell Matt, *as if hearing it once again would make a dent in his denial,* that he was ill and needed professional help. And yet, all three knew that Matt was not going to follow up with the clinic appointment.

They could have talked about that with Matt directly. But to do that they would have had to make it safe for him to talk, not let fear rule the conversation, and stop pushing their agenda.

3. Stop Pushing Their Agenda?

Matt was about to leave yet another hospitalization, and his parents and doctor knew he would not follow through with their recommendations because he never had before. But that didn't stop the three of them from pushing their hopeless agenda anyway. Dr. Greene wanted to communicate the details of the post-hospital treatment plans and "seal the deal" so to speak (even though he admitted to me later that he knew Matt would never follow through with the plan as it had been presented to him). Matt wanted to leave the hospital and was willing, if that's what it took, to take medicine for the time being. How long he was willing to stay on the medicine was never determined because Matt did not trust his doctor or parents enough to be forthcoming and reveal what his true feelings were. Mr. Blackburn openly predicted that his son would stay on the medicine for less than one week while Brian naively hoped that Matt would be willing to follow doctor's orders for months to come.

Mr. Blackburn was pursuing an agenda, which was trying to convince Brian to hold Matt in the hospital longer. And although Mrs. Blackburn was focused on the same agenda, she was preoccupied with her guilt and with not wanting to hurt or anger Matt. And what was Matt's agenda? No one asked, so we really don't know, although I found out later.

4. Let It Be?

Matt was not offering his opinion or saying he would not take his pills. At least not directly. So there was little in the meeting for his doctor and parents to react to. But his parents were reacting to things Matt had said and done in the past. His father was angry from the start, not only because the hospital was discharging his son, whom he felt was too ill to come home, but also because he didn't believe Matt was telling the truth. When Matt said he'd go to his appointment and take his medicine, his father reacted essentially by calling him a liar ("That's what you promised us before, but when we get home you disappear into your room and you don't go anywhere."). Although more subtle, Matt's mother also reacted to his reassurances with disbelief.

5. Respect What They'd Heard?

No one echoed back to Matt what they understood him to be saying. Matt's views on whether he was ill and needed treatment were not respected. There was at least one missed opportunity. When Matt said, "this time is different," his doctor or parents could have replied, "So, Matt, I want to understand. You're saying this time is different. Is that right?" If such a question had been asked, not with anger or sarcasm, but with genuine curiosity, Matt would have answered yes, his defenses would have dropped a notch, and he would have told them something very important. This time really was different for him. He truly did not want to come back to the hospital ever again, certainly not the way he had this time (his parents had called the police, who brought him to the hospital against his will). And if they had echoed back what they heard and Matt had felt they truly understood, a problem they all shared could have been identified. They could have worked together to keep him out of the hospital. From Matt's perspective his parents were the reason, from their perspective it was the mental illness. But they all agreed that no one wanted him to end up in the hospital again (even the insurance company would have agreed to that!). This was a missed opportunity to help Matt drop his defenses and turn down the volume on everyone's anger.Let me give you a feel for what I am talking about.

Brian was Matt's doctor, and I was Brian's supervisor, so sometimes I met with the two of them together. During one of these meetings, Matt had described the terror he felt when the police brought him to the hospital. He had never felt so scared before. He never wanted to feel that way again. And he had grown tired of being hospitalized again and again. I asked him why he thought his parents had called the police, and he answered "because they think I'm sick."

"But that doesn't tell me *why* they would put you through this."

"They think I'm sick and need to be in the looney bin, that's why."

"Let me ask the question differently. What's motivating them to do this to you? Do they hate you?"

"No."

"Do they want to hurt you?"

"I don't know. I don't think so."

"Then why would they call the police on their son?"

"They're afraid, I guess."

"Matt, let me see if I have this right. Your parents called the police to bring you to the hospital against your will not because they hate you or want to hurt you but because they're afraid. Do I have that right?"

"Yeah. That's it."

"What are they afraid about?"

"They're afraid I'll get hurt."

"Now, I know you disagree with them on this, but before we talk about that let me see if I am following you so far. Your parents were afraid you would get hurt so they wanted you in the hospital to keep you safe. Is that right?" He nodded. "What does that tell you about how your mom and dad feel about you?"

"They love me."

"So you have a big problem here don't you. How do you convince your parents to stop throwing you in the hospital? I mean, you can't convince them to stop loving you, can you?"

"No," he said smiling.

"Then what?"

"I can't convince them there's nothing wrong with me. You guys have all brainwashed them!" We both laughed at his reminder that people like me, doctors, were at the root of his problem.

"No. And they can't convince you that you're sick. So there you are. What could you work on together?"

"I guess reassuring them so they don't get scared and call the police."

"How can you do that?"

"There's nothing I could do to convince them."

"Nothing?"

"Well, no, not nothing. I could take the medicine."

"But if I understand you, you're not sick. Why would you take medicine if there's nothing wrong with you?"

"To keep them off my back!" he said laughing.

This conversation, though valuable, would have been priceless had Matt had it with his parents. But because they were afraid and unable to echo what they heard, they missed a chance to find common ground with their son and work on the problem they all agreed Matt had (i.e., hospitalizations against his will were bad). By redefining the problem so that it was no longer about the question of whether or not he was sick and needed help, and clarifying that he knew his "misguided" parents were motivated by love, Matt could have translated the impossible problem he had into one that was workable.

6. Find Workable Problems?

When it came to defining the problem, Matt, his parents, and Dr. Greene were talking apples and oranges. Matt saw the problem as his parents, the police who listened to them, and the shrinks who had convinced his mother and father he was ill. His parents and Dr. Greene saw the problem as Matt's being stubborn, immature, and defensive. He was not taking any responsibility for the illness he *clearly* had. On the other hand, Matt and I had easily found at least one workable problem. We agreed that the only problem anyone would be willing to work on with him was how to keep him out of the hospital.

Identifying a problem we could work on together opened up a way for us to work as allies rather than adversaries. After his parents left, I briefly met with Matt and Dr. Greene I said: "Well you know it's your choice, Matt. You know what I think, and I can't force you to do something you don't believe in. I wouldn't want to do that even if I could, unless, of course, you were in danger, which you're not in right now. I respect your right to make this decision for yourself. I know you told Dr. Greene and your parents that you would stay on the medicine. But if you change your mind, and if I had to guess I'd guess you will since you don't believe you're sick, I hope you will pay close attention to what happens next. It's your life. Don't just have an opinion about the medication; prove to yourself whether your opinion is right or wrong."

"I already said I'd take the pills!" he responded defensively, probably because I was implying that I didn't believe the reassurances he'd given Dr. Greene and his parents.

"Okay, I will take you at your word. But I have to say that if it were me, I wouldn't take the medicine." Seeing that Brian looked mortified by what I had just said, I asked him, "Dr. Greene, do you have something to say? You look like you might have a different view on this."

"Well, I don't think you really meant that if you were in Matt's shoes you wouldn't take the medicine."

"That's exactly what I meant." Brian frowned and seemed to be searching for words when Matt saved him by asking me, "So, you don't think I need the drugs?"

"I didn't say that. What I said is that if I were you I wouldn't take them after I leave the hospital. Matt, you don't believe you have a mental illness and you feel strongly you shouldn't be taking medicine for an illness you don't have. That sounds like common sense to me. Who would take pills if they didn't think they needed them? What would be the point? If I believed those things I wouldn't be planning on taking the medicine when people were no longer looking over my shoulder. If I were in your shoes, I would say what it took to get out of here and then follow my own compass. Isn't that really where you are? You can tell me and you will still go home today. It won't change a thing."

"I would never do that," Matt said facetiously, a smile spreading across his face. I smiled back as we both recognized and shared the truth of what he would do once the door closed behind him.

"Hypothetically then, if you do stop taking the medicine, ask yourself these three questions: What stays the same? What gets worse? What gets better? Write it down like we've been doing while you were here. You know what I mean?"

"Yeah. The pluses and minuses."

"Exactly. So you know what I'm talking about?"

"Yeah. It's my life. I hold the key and it's up to me to decide."

"Right. Now, you've decided you really don't want to take the medicine, right?"

"Yeah," he admitted sheepishly. "But I will anyway. Everyone wants me to, so I will."

"Well, I don't know if everyone wants you to, but you know my opinion. I hope that you will. But if you decide to stop, I want you to know I respect that this is your life and your right."

"Yeah, but you'll think I'm stupid."

"No, I won't. But I might think you made a bad decision if you made an uninformed decision."

"You're the doctor, you would know."

"That's not what I meant. You are in the best position to be the expert on this issue. Be a scientist. Think of this as an experiment. Collect the data. Don't jump to conclusions one way or the other. Just pay attention to what happens when you're not taking the medicine. Ask people you trust how you seem when you're off medicine. Think you'd be interested in doing that?"

"I don't know. I already know the answer."

"Well, it seems everyone else already thinks they know the answer, too, and most of them disagree with you. Here's your chance to prove them wrong."

"I'll try to keep an open mind."

"That's all I'm suggesting. Anything else you want to talk about before we stop? Any feedback for me?"

"No, I guess not."

"Well, good luck." I stood up, extended my hand, and added, "I hope I never see you again."

"Same here," Matt replied. We both laughed as we shook hands. If I saw Matt, it would be because he was back in the hospital. Keeping him out of the hospital and in his life was something we both wholeheartedly agreed upon.

7. Remember the Headlines?

No one appeared to pay attention to the headlines, much less write them down. Of course, writing down what Matt had to say would have been awkward in this situation because his doctor and parents had never practiced this technique with him. It's true that Brian often took notes during their sessions, but they were almost entirely about symptoms he was observing. He rarely recorded Matt's subjective experience of the problem (his parents, the police, and the "shrinks") or statements that revealed what was important to him, what motivated him (staying out of the hospital, getting a job and a place of his own). But it would have been easy to ask, "Is it alright with you if I write down what you're telling us is most important to you?"

Effective Listening

Dr. Ivan Kohut, a third-year resident in psychiatry, was meeting with Vicky, the forty-five year old woman with manic depression you heard about in Chapter 2. Her husband, Scott was also present. Vicky had spent the last two weeks in the hospital following a manic episode during which she took her two children on a three-day road-trip to Mount Desert Island National Park in Maine.

The first night of the trip was especially disturbing because Scott had no idea where his family had gone until Vicky called him at 11:00 p.m. to explain that she wanted their children to experience the same spiritual awakening she was having. God had instructed her to take them to the top of Cadillac Mountain because it was the highest point on the East coast, and had told her that once they were there he would come to them.

Having gone through two previous manic episodes with Vicky over the course of their marriage, Scott figured out what was happening much more quickly than he had in the past. During the phone call he begged her to come home, but she refused, and when he told her he thought she was becoming sick, she abruptly hung up the phone. Scott immediately called the police in the area she had phoned from, but they told him there wasn't much they could do except to "keep an eye out for her car." They suggested he call the National Park Headquarters in Maine. With the help of Vicky's psychiatrist, Scott was able to convince the Park Rangers to intercept his wife when she arrived. He then flew up to Maine, and after much cajoling and threats of commitment, she agreed to return to New York and go to the hospital. From both Scott's and Vicky's perspective the drive back was nightmarish. The children, as children often do, were unconsciously running interference by misbehaving. Their fights and tantrums together with Vicky's rapid-fire speech and grandiose proclamations made for an excruciatingly long drive home.

After greeting the couple, Ivan sat down and began by asking, "What would the two of you like to talk about today? I have two things I'd like to put on our agenda. How about you, Vicky?"

"When do I get out of here? That's the only thing I'd like to talk about."

"Okay. Scott, how about you?"

"Well, I have the same question. And I also want to talk about her medications."

"Anything else? Either of you?"

"No," Vicky answered quickly.

Scott thought a minute, then said, "I suppose not, maybe more will occur to me as we talk."

"Good. My two agenda items are similar. I want to report on how I think Vicky is doing and then ask her how she feels about the discharge plan. So that's basically three items: One, when does Vicky get out of here; two, my view on how she's doing, and three, Vicky's opinion of the plan we put together for after she leaves. If it's okay with the two of you, I'd like to get the second item out of the way first." Vicky and Scott both nodded their approval. Addressing Vicky, Ivan said, "I think you are doing much better than when we first met two weeks ago. Back then you were sleeping about two to four hours a night, your thoughts were racing, your speech was pressured, you were euphoric, extremely irritable, and you had some unusual thoughts about God and supernatural abilities you felt he had given you. Right now your sleep is back to normal, your thoughts aren't racing, and your speech isn't pressured. You don't need me to describe your mood. How would you describe your mood over the last week?"

"Kind of constricted. I'm not as happy and I don't get irritated so easily. I'm not depressed."

"Do you miss the happy feeling?"

"You know I do, Dr. Kohut! Wouldn't you?"

"Absolutely." Noting the smile on her face, he added, "But it looks to me like you can still feel happy. It's the extreme happiness, the high, that's gone. Yes?"

"That's true," she answered.

"So, in a nutshell, I think you're ready to go home the day after tomorrow."

Vicky looked surprised and said, "Well, that answers my question. Why didn't you tell me that this morning when we met?"

"I suppose you don't remember, but I told you I had to discuss it with the team first. I wanted everyone's input. We generally make these decisions by consensus, and the consensus is that you're much improved and can go home. Scott, any opinion about this?"

"Not really. I expected it. I see that she's getting back to normal. But I guess I'm not clear on what happens next. What about the medications, and what can we do to keep this from happening again?"

"Good segue to the last item on our agenda — what happens next with respect to your treatment." Ivan answered, addressing Vicky once again. "I'd like to see you in the clinic once a week for the next couple of months, and then maybe drop down to once a month. I don't want to change anything about the medication you're taking right now. I'd like to see how you do over the next couple of weeks, then re-evaluate and discuss if we should make any adjustments. What are your thoughts about what should happen next?"

Vicky laughed and asked, "Does it really matter? Everyone thinks I should stay on medication."

"Of course it matters!" Scott replied, a little irritated and defensive.

"You're the boss here, even if it doesn't seem that way now," Ivan added.

"What are you talking about?" Vicky asked.

"I am talking about the fact that what your husband and I think you should do doesn't amount to a hill of beans compred to what you think you should do. If you believe that the medications have done their job and want to stop taking them, you will. I can't stop you and neither can your husband."

"Then why am I in this hospital? I don't feel like the boss."

"That's because you lost a lot of control when the bipolar disorder you have flared up. It caused you to do things that worried a lot of people and motivated them to take control away from you. But now you've got the illness under control again and you're back in the driver's seat."

"If that's true, then I don't want to take these drugs for more than a month or two."

"So, if I understand you, you don't want to take these drugs for more than two months at the most. Right?"

"Yes."

"Okay."

"Wait a minute!" Scott interrupted. "That's how she got into this mess in the first place. Every doctor she's seen, including you, has told us she will very likely have to stay on these medications for the rest of her life."

"If she doesn't want to have another flare-up, yes, that's true. That is my opinion. Also, the medications will help to keep her from becoming depressed again. I'm not contradicting myself. I'm saying something else. It's Vicky's choice, not yours or mine. But the choices you make," he added, looking at Vicky, "will have consequences."

"You make it sound so ominous," she replied.

"I think the consequences of stopping your treatment will be very negative. You know what my professional recommendation is and what your last psychiatrist felt. You know what your husband and your family would like. But what you believe is what you will ultimately do. And I have to respect that. But I am curious about one thing. Why don't you think you will need the medications? Just this morning you told me they've been very helpful over the past few weeks. Were you just 'yessing' me or did you really mean it?"

"I meant it. They've done their job. But I'm better now."

"So you see yourself as cured of bipolar disorder," Ivan stated.

"Well, I'm not sure I have manic depression. But whatever was going on, yes, the medications helped calm me down. So,yes. The problem is solved. Why would I want to be on these drugs for the rest of my life when the problem doesn't exist anymore?"

"So what you're saying," Ivan began, "is that you had some kind of problem, not manic depression, that the drugs helped you with. And now that the problem is solved, you don't want to keep taking the medication. Right?"

"Right."

"Want my opinion on what you just said?"

"I already know it."

"Actually, it may surprise you."

"Shoot."

"What you propose is certainly possible." Ivan said to the couples' surprise. "How about we make a deal. If you decide, six months from now, that you still want to go off your medications, we can give it a try. But I won't have any part of it if we're not meeting regularly."

"Why would you do that? You already told me you think I have to stay on these medications forever."

"Because your opinion is the only one that ultimately determines whether or not you stay in treatment. I am willing to work with you to prove what you believe even though I don't believe it. I have only two requirements: that you see me regularly, and that you keep a daily diary during the time we're lowering your dosages."

"Why a diary?"

"So you have a record of how you were thinking and acting during the time your medication was lowered. It will also help you to pay attention to the consequences, not only for you but for your family."

"I would be willing to do that," Vicky replied.

"Okay, then let's write the deal down so we all remember. You will stay on the medications for another six months. If at that time you still want to discontinue the drugs, we do it together," he said aloud as he wrote down his words. Then he added as an afterthought, "I'd like to include Scott in some of those meetings as well if that's okay."

"Sure," she answered.

"And if we go that route, you will keep a daily diary. We can talk more about what I'd like you to record—cross that bridge when we come to it. Do I have it right? Is this what we agreed to?"

"Yes," both Vicky and Scott replied.

1. Make It Safe

Did Ivan make it safe for Vicky to talk? Yes. He made it clear that he wanted to hear Vicky's views on the treatment and was actually reluctant to tell her his views, which she already knew. She understood she could talk about her belief that she was not sick and didn't need medicine without her doctor's contradicting her. She also knew that Ivan would keep her husband from jumping down her throat. Ivan made it clear that her opinion was the only one that really mattered at the moment. It was more important than his and Scott's opinion.

2. Know Your Fears

Scott got nervous and went on the attack for a moment when Ivan acknowledged, without argument, Vicky's desire to stop taking the medicine. Otherwise, Scott did a great job of listening passively as his wife and doctor discussed her views on the problem and what she needed. In previous meetings Ivan had worked with Scott to help him recognize where he was powerless and where he had power. Where he was powerless was in convincing his wife she had manic-depression and needed to be on medication for the rest of her life. He hadn't succeeded in four years, and Ivan helped him to recognize what was obvious: He wasn't going to suddenly succeed now by continuing the argument. Where he had power was in repairing their relationship so that she would feel he was once again her ally, on her team, and that they were working on the same problems together.

Ivan was clear about his fears and understood that he had nothing to lose by listening to Vicky's views. He knew he would not harm her by allowing her to be honest, by not contradicting her views without her permission (he always asked her if he could give his opinion before he gave it), and by actively listening.

3. Stop Pushing Your Agenda

Not only did they agree on an agenda, but over the course of their conversation Ivan repeatedly checked back with Vicky and her husband to ensure that there wasn't anything else either of them wanted to talk about. The main agenda was understanding Vicky's views and working with how she experienced all this.

4. Let it Be

Ivan did not react emotionally to Vicky's statement that she wanted to stop taking medication. Neither did Scott, except during the one brief moment when his fears caught him off guard. Neither Ivan nor Scott jumped in with their opinions to refute Vicky's statement that she was no longer ill and planned to stop taking the medication. They let her opinions stand. They respected her point of view. When Ivan did offer his opinion, he empowered Vicky by first asking if it was okay with her for him to tell her what he thought.

5. Respect What You've Heard

Ivan did this repeatedly, often rephrasing things Vicky had said to ensure that he "got it right." He prefaced his reflective statements by indicating that he just wanted to be sure he understood her correctly ("Let me see if I got this right?"), used her words without comment or criticism, and then asked her if he'd understood correctly. He acknowledged that he understood and genuinely respected her point of view.

6. Find Workable Problems

Vicky felt that the medications were a short-term treatment, like antibiotics for an infection, rather than a long-term treatment, like insulin for diabetes. The good news is that Vicky had some insight, nowhere near as much as her family and doctor would have liked, but enough to work with. She understood that the drugs helped her when she had symptoms. However, she didn't understand that the drugs could also prevent the symptoms from returning when she was feeling well.

Now that she was feeling well, Vicky wanted to stop taking the medicines. Although Ivan understood that statistically it was highly unlikely she could stop without getting sick again, there was a very, very, small chance that she could. He also understood that until the day Vicky "owned" the treatment, until she found a reason that made sense to *her* to stay on the medicine, she never would. Her problem, which he was willing to help her with for the time being, was taking the medicine. But he would work with her on this only if she stayed in therapy with him, allowed Scott to come to some of the sessions, and took responsibility for tracking what happened when she stopped taking the medicine. By agreeing to work with her on the problem as she defined it, he kept her in therapy and on the medication for a longer period of time than if he had insisted the treatment was "a life sentence," as she had once described it. He also laid the foundation for her discovering reasons to continue in treatment.

7. Remember the Headlines

Ivan not only wrote down what they had agreed to do about the medications but asked permission to do so before starting. This was important because it emphasized Ivan's wish to collaborate rather than pontificate. By asking, he also underscored that Vicky would be in charge after she left the hospital. He wasn't afraid to acknowledge his own powerlessness. By doing that, he reminded Vicky that the choice to continue treatment was hers, as was the responsibility for the consequences that would follow her decision. The headlines were that she wanted off the medications and that she understood they helped her when her thoughts were racing, when she wasn't sleeping, and when she got tired out (these were the things she saw as problems even though she didn't think she had an illness).

Listening is an active process. It involves asking many questions and not reacting to what you are hearing. You should think of yourself as a scientist trying to unravel a mystery. Your task is to gain a clear idea of what *your loved one's* experience of the illness and treatment is. Once you know how he experiences the idea of having a mental illness and taking psychiatric drugs you will have acquired vital knowledge you need in order to build a treatment agreement.

The Danger of Listening Reflectively

Very likely the person you are listening to reflectively and without judgment will make the mistake of thinking you believe what he is telling you (about not being sick, not needing medications, or the CIA conspiracy). He may ask you to help him catch the CIA in the act or talk to his parents so he can go off medications since you seem to agree he doesn't need them. I touch on this problem at various points in this book—it's why most people are afraid of reflective listening---but let me introduce you to two new tools: *The Delaying Tool* and the *Three A's For Giving Your Opinion* that will allow you to use reflective listening without falling prey to these traps. I will talk about these both again later, but let me lay it out for you here concisely.

The Delaying Tool

You want to delay giving your opinion about controversial topics (delusions, desire to not take medicine, etc.) for as long as possible to first preserve the alliance you are building, delay the hurt your answer will cause and perhaps most importantly, shift the locus of control onto the person who is asking for your opinion. After all, when you give it, he has no one to blame for hearing your point of view but himself, especially if you have delayed giving it because you have been genuinely reluctant to do so. So, in terms of learning to LEAP, the longer you are able to delay giving your opinion, the more the other person will have experienced you as respecting his and, therefore, the more obligated he will feel to respect yours (or at least hear you out.) If he has to solicit it, the more in control he will feel and, therefore, the less defensive he will be when he hears it. And the harder he has to work for it, the more it will matter when you finally do give it. For these three reasons, your opinion will have more weight.

When you delay, try the following: first *honor the question* by promising to answer, *try and change the topic* and *ask permission* to do so. Here are some examples that include all three elements (the promise, the diversion and the request for permission to change the topic):

I promise I will tell you whether I think you are sick. But first, if it's OK with you, I would like to hear more about _____ . Would that be all right?

I will answer you question about the CIA. Can I ask you to give me some more details about what happened last night first? Would that be OK?

You've asked me many times whether I think you are delusional. I promise to answer. But if its OK with you, before I tell you what I see, could you tell me more about_____?

I promise to answer your question about whether you should stop taking medicine. Before I do, I want you to know that I think your opinon about this is far more important than mind. So can you tell me all the reasons why you want to do that?

The "A" Tools for Giving your Opinion

Sometimes, even after you've listened and empathized, the other person won't ask you what you think. This is rare in my experience, and if it happens to you I want you to consider two possibilities. One is that you have not used the tools you've learned as effectively as you could and the other is that the person likes talking so much that he simply isn't interested in what you have to say. If it's the latter, you can ask if he or she would be interested in hearing your perspective. You can say something like, "After listening to you, I have a much better picture of your views on this. Can I tell you what *I* think?" I've never heard of anyone who'd used the listening and empathy tools receiving a "no" in answer to this question, and I don't believe you will either.

But whether you have been asked for your opinion repeatedly and delayed giving it, or you have had to offer it because the person—despite being cooled down and feeling listened to and respected—doesn't ask, the *way* you deliver your opinion will determine whether it throws more fuel on the fire or continues to douse the flames. If you want to get past the impasse, there are three new tools you now need to add to your tool belt. I often use all three of them together, but sometimes you need only one or two to get the job done. I call these my "A" tools both to make them easier to remember and because they are A-list powerful tools you can use whenever you're arguing or negotiating.

I like to think of these tools as soft like felt or like a goose down pillow. Sometimes I think of them as airbags. In other words, they are tools that help to soften the blow and save lives— or at least relationships. The three As are *apologize, acknowledge,* and *agree.*

APOLOGIZE

Apologizing may be the last thing you think you need or want to do at this point. After all, the other person has been asking you (probably more than once) what you think. You're only doing what she's asked. In fact, you may think that if you need to apologize for anything it would be for having delayed so long. But that's not the way it works.

Keep in mind the reason you delayed in the first place: because you're aware that when you do give your opinion it's likely to damage the trust you've so carefully been building. When you finally admit that you really still don't agree, the other person is likely to be disappointed, to feel somehow betrayed, and to get angry all over again. So what you need to indicate is that you understand all this and you apologize, because you truly wish that what you believe didn't make her feel that way.

Notice that I'm *not* suggesting you apologize for the opinion you're about to offer (e.g., Yes I think you probably do have bipolar disorder), just for the feelings it might engender. You're not saying *I'm sorry I feel this way* but rather *I'm sorry that what I have to say may make* you *feel such and such.* What you might say is something like, "Before I tell you what I think about this, I want to apologize because what I think might feel hurtful or disappointing."

Understanding that difference ought to make the process easier for you, but if you still feel unable to apologize, you're probably still too angry, and you need to take a few deep breaths, step back, if only for a moment, and think about why you're doing this in the first place.

And when you do apologize, just be sure that you *don't* use the word "but," as in, "I apologize if this is going to upset you, *but*, I think..." I mentioned this but want to emphasize it here again because it is so important. People who are in a disagreement typically stop listening when they hear the word "but." It's as if you had pushed a button on a remote control and shut off their hearing aid. Not only are they incapable of hearing you; but the most likely outcome is that you'll just revert to "butting" heads all over again.

ACKNOWLEDGE

What is it that you need to acknowledge? Certainly not that you still think you're right (although, ultimately, that's more or less what you're going to be saying). Rather, you need to acknowledge that you're not infallible and you might be wrong– even though you clearly don't think so. (And you're *not* going to say *that!*)So, after you apologize, say something like, "Also, I could be wrong about this. I don't know everything."

When you do that you are, first of all, indicating that you are flexible. If you can be flexible, you're more likely to trigger some flexibility in the other person. If you're rigid and dogmatic, you're equally likely to trigger that. Remember that LEAP is all about giving in order to get.

Acknowledging that you could possibly be wrong is also a way to convey respect because you are not insisting that you are wise and the other person is ignorant. It's the same principal Benjamin Franklin wrote about in his autobiography --when he said, "I made it a rule to forbear all direct contradiction to the sentiment of others, and all positive assertion of my own. I even forbade myself the use of every word or expression in the language that imported a fix'd opinion...for these fifty years past no one has ever heard a dogmatical expression escape me." If it worked for Benjamin Franklin, who broke many seemingly insurmountable impasses, it can work for you.

AGREE

I've already said that you're not going to be agreeing with the other person's opinion. So what is this about? Here, you're going to ask her to agree that you disagree. In other words, you'll be indicating that you respect her opinion and hope that she'll respect yours: "I hope we can just agree to disagree on this. I respect your point of view and I won't try to talk you out of it. I hope you can respect mine."

Using the three "A" tools is far easier than it might appear at first glance. When my brother Henry asked me if I thought he had schizophrenia I said: "I'm sorry because this might hurt your feelings. I want you to know I could be wrong, I don't know everything, but yes, I think you might have schizophrenia. I hope we don't have to argue about this: I respect your opinion on this and I hope you respect mine. Let's just disagree on this." Did you see the 3 A's?

Here is a shorter example. "Should you take the medicine? I'm sorry I feel this way and I could be wrong, I just hope we can agree to disagree on this. Yes I think you ought to try it for at least a few months and see how it goes."

The point is to be humble, help the person save face and preserve the relationship you've been building. Remember, you will win on the strength of your relationship rather than on the strength of your argument.

7
Empathize

A few years after he first became ill, my brother and I were talking about one of his medications, Haldol. He hated Haldol (a.k.a. haloperidol) because it made him feel "stiff" and "groggy." As I listened to his complaints, I understood for the first time some of the frustration he felt about taking these medications. I recall saying something along the lines of, "I can see why you don't like these drugs. They make feel stiff and groggy." The conversation stands out in my mind because for the first time we were calmly talking and listening to one another *about the medication* instead of arguing.

Usually our conversations on this topic were a disaster. I would hold my ground and pontificate about why he must take the medications prescribed for him and about how immature it was of him not to accept the fact that he was ill. Brothers can often be that way. But after working for a year as a therapy aide on an inpatient psychiatric ward, I was beginning to learn how important it was to listen. As I listened, I couldn't help beginning to empathize. I love Henry, and when someone you love is in pain, it's hard not to empathize. Learning to listen led to empathy. And my empathy ultimately resulted in my brother's showing a real interest in *my thoughts* about the illness he felt he did not have and the medications he was sure he did not need.

These are among the most important feelings to connect with because they are the feelings that drive people with mental illness away from their loved ones and therapists.

When you feel empathy and convey it, your loved one will very likely feel understood and respected. Whenever you convey that you understand how your loved one is feeling, his or her defensiveness will decrease and openness to your opinion will increase. If you have followed the advice I gave in the previous chapter, if you have listened reflectively to your loved one's experience of his illness and the prescribed treatment, you will naturally begin to empathize. But communicating your empathy can be tricky when you're talking to someone who has a psychotic illness. Many people worry that they should not empathize with certain feelings, such as anger about being forced to take medicine, fear of treatment, or feelings connected to delusions. In fact, these are among the most important feelings to connect with because they are the feelings that drive people with mental illness away from their loved ones and therapists.

Conveying empathy

You must first learn what it is you should be empathizing with. The short answer is just about any feeling your loved one is willing to reveal. But there are certain feelings that are particularly important for you to understand. Whether they are rational ("I am so sick and tired of everybody telling me I am sick!") or irrational ("The C.I.A. has implanted microchips in the capsules so they can track me!"), you want to be sure to empathize with:

- **Frustrations** (about pressure from others to take medication and about personal goals that have not been met).
- **Fears** (about medication, being stigmatized, and failing).
- **Discomfort** (attributed to medications, such as gaining weight or feeling groggy, slowed down, less creative, stiff, etc.).
- **Desires** (to work, get married, have children, return to school, stay out of the hospital, etc.).

A magical thing happens when you combine reflective listening with empathy. Your loved one will ask you what you think! I can almost guarantee this will happen. For example, remember the conversation I had with Matt and his doctor? Matt, who everyone knew didn't think he was mentally ill, had just insincerely promised to take his medicine when he left the hospital. And I said "Okay. I will take you at your word. But I have to say that if it were me, I wouldn't take the medicine." He opened up to me then and was more honest about not wanting to take the drugs. When he did that, I focused on empathizing with his feelings about taking them. I said "You sound angry that everyone is pushing these drugs on you. Are you?" He agreed, then eventually asked me, "So, you don't think I need the drugs?" You saw my answer to that question, but what you didn't know was that the time was ripe for me to give him my opinion. He was about to leave the hospital, and it was my last chance to talk with him. Most of the time, however, when someone asks my opinion about a delusion, about whether I think he's mentally ill, or if he needs medications, I delay answering as long as possible. For example, one patient was convinced that his mother was poisoning his food. I listened and empathized, and he then asked me if I believed it was actually happening. Our conversation about this began with my saying, "So, if I understand you correctly, you mother has been poisoning your food. Do I have that right?"

"Yes!"

"How do you feel about that?"

"Are you serious?! How would you feel?"

"I would feel, and I think anyone would feel, scared and angry," I replied.

"So, do you believe it? Are you going to do something about it?" he asked.

I didn't answer his questions at that point, although I did later. I delayed answering as long as I could. I will be getting to the reasons for that and explain how you can delay answering without frustrating the questioner. For now, however, the take home point is: Listen and empathize and you will be asked your opinion. And that is ultimately what you want to have happen because an opinion that has been asked for carries far more weight than one that is forced on a person who is arguing with you.

Dolores

Dolores, who has had schizophrenia for nearly 20 years, told me that she didn't need medication or a day treatment program because there was nothing wrong with her. What did Dolores feel she needed? More than anything else, she wanted a job. She was frustrated that she did not have a job and with her family, who told her she couldn't work. Her family was being reasonably pessimistic. The fact is that Dolores had been unable to keep a job for more than a few days at a time and she had been employed only a handful of times over the past twenty years.

By the time I met her, Dolores, like many individuals with serious mental illness who don't know they're ill, had been hospitalized many times. In her case, it was about two to four times a year. Although she almost always signed herself into the hospital voluntarily, she would do this only after receiving tremendous pressure from her family. When I talked with her about what she planned to do when she left the hospital this time, she told me simply, "Get a job."

If you were her therapist and discussing her plans, you might be tempted (as I was early in my career) to focus on the irrationality of that idea. After all, she had a long history of poor adherence to her medication regimen, and there was no reason to believe that her long-standing pattern of unemployment was about to change. You would understandably think that talking about her reluctance to stay in treatment would be more beneficial to her than encouraging or agreeing with her irrational plan for herself.

The problem was, Dolores had absolutely no interest in talking about drugs, day treatment programs, or doctor's appointments. Would you want to talk about those things if you were not ill? So, instead of going that route, I began our talk about her plans for the future by empathizing with what she was feeling at that moment.

"You want to get a job when you leave?"

"I'm going to work on Wall Street," she answered quickly.

"Why Wall Street?" I asked, ignoring for now how far-fetched her plan was.

"I want to make a lot of money. I need to have my own money."

"It's important to you to have your own money and you can do that by working on Wall Street. Is that right?" I reflected back to her.

"Yes. I hate having to ask my family for money."

"How come?"

"It makes me feel like a child. My little sister [who was in her thirties] is a stockbroker and you should see her house. I'm the big sister; I should be making money too!"

"It sounds like asking for money makes you feel embarrassed or even a little humiliated. Am I right about that?" I asked, checking to see if I understood her feelings and at the same time communicating my empathy.

"It does. Wouldn't you be embarrassed?" she asked.

"Yes, I think I probably would feel that way." Sensing an opening, I added, "Can I ask you something?"

"What?"

Careful not to add to her humiliation and raise her defenses, I asked, "Why do you think you haven't worked very much?" (Note that I didn't ask, "Why is it you've only worked about twelve days in your entire adult life?"). She quickly answered, "Because I'm always in the damn hospital!"

"Is being in the hospital keeping you from work?"

"I'm angry about being in the hospital so much. I want to get on with my life and I can't if I'm in a damn hospital."

"So it's much more than frustration you feel. It makes you angry. Yes?" I asked, nodding my head.

"Very angry," she answered more calmly.

Pushing ahead, I asked, "How do you feel about the fact that it's been hard to find work?"

"Sometimes I want to scream!"

"That sounds infuriating. Is it?"

"No. It is frustrating," she answered, correcting my misperception.

"So it's frustrating. Sorry I got that wrong."

"That's okay," she reassured me.

During this brief exchange, I empathized with Dolores's feelings of *humiliation*, her deep *desire* to work, and her *frustration* with being unable to work. Did you notice that nearly everything I said was in the form of a question? That is how you should do reflective listening. Also, by making a statement about my understanding of her feelings and asking if I had it right, I was able to make sure I understood what she meant when she said she wanted to scream. I also communicated my empathy for what she was feeling and allowed her to be in control of the conversation.

Also, by asking questions instead of commenting on what she had to say ("What you're planning isn't realistic."), I learned what was important to Dolores, what was uppermost on her mind, and how she was feeling. By doing that, I created a window of opportunity, which I later used to discuss what role, if any, she felt treatment might play in what she wanted to accomplish (i.e., staying out of the hospital and working on Wall Street).

Whenever you want to facilitate change in another person, you must first become his friend (i.e., someone he trusts). Whenever you convey empathy for another person's experience, he feels understood, respected, and more trusting. Because you understand the other person's point of view and how he feels about his situation, there is nothing to argue about. Consequently, he becomes less defensive and more open to hearing your perspective. And, more often than not, he will ask either: "So do you believe me?" Or, "Why are you acting like you believe me? You don't believe me, do you?" These questions are opposite sides of the same coin. And it's a coin you want to handle carefully as it is vital to where you want to go.

How to handle the "Do you agree with me?" question

Delay answering questions about delusions, having a mental illness, or the need for medication as long as you can. There are two reasons to do this. First, so that you preserve and build on the good relationship you have been creating with reflective listening and empathy. Up this point the person feels that his or her opinion has been respected and honored. In fact, he feels so certain of your respect for his opinion that he has made the mistake of thinking you probably agree with him. Therefore, when you do give your opinion, it will probably hurt and make the person defensive. The longer you wait, the more experiences he will have of your listening to him without disagreeing or, essentially, telling him he's "crazy," which is just how many persons with mental illness will hear your opinion unless you pay close attention to how you give it.

The second reason to delay has to do with the two ways one can give an opinion that I told you about in the previous chapter. By making the person ask you repeatedly for your opinion, you make him responsible for having to hear it. Think about it. If you asked me over and over again whether I thought you were mentally ill and needed medication, and I didn't seem very eager to tell you, you'd have no one to blame but yourself for having coerced me into giving it. Try to remember:

- Only give your opinion when it has been asked for
- An opinion that has been asked for carries more weight than an unsolicited opinion
- It is important to avoid or delay giving your opinion

So how can you delay giving your opinion on these matters that are so important to your loved one? In the space below, I want you to write down something you could say to delay giving your opinion on the question, "Do you think I am mentally ill and need to take medicine?"

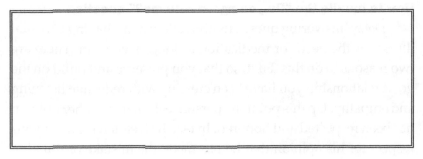

Read what you wrote and imagine it was being said to you. How would you feel about it?

The trick to delaying is first to honor the question by promising to answer it. By doing that, you empower the person by asking his permission to delay answering and you make the point that *his opinion is more important* than yours. It is not as complicated as it sounds. Here are some examples.

- "I promise I will answer your question, but, if it's okay with you, I want to wait and listen to you some more first, okay?"
- "I will tell you, but I would rather keep listening to your views on this because I am learning a lot about you I didn't know. Can I tell you later what I think?"

- "You know, your opinion is the most important opinion in this room, not mine. So I would like to learn more before I tell you what I think, if that's alright with you."

I once had a patient say to me, "But you're the doctor! Your opinion has got to be more important than mine." I disagreed and I told him so. "When we're done talking and you walk out this door, you are in the driver's seat. Your opinion is what will determine what you do and where you go, the choices you make. Not mine. So you're opinion is far more important than mine." By saying this, I was empowering him while humbling myself. More important, it was coming from my heart. I believed it. As you can imagine, this made me and my opinion a lot less threatening to him than I or it would have been otherwise.

When you feel the time is right, you want to give your opinion.

At some point, when you feel the time is right, you want to give your opinion. Earlier in the book I told you about the research that indicates how a special kind of relationship can influence someone's willingness to take medicine. That relationship is one in which the mentally ill person feels that his opinion is respected, trusts the other person, and believes that this other person thinks taking medicine is a very good idea. Well, now is your chance to give your opinion. But, for the same reasons you delayed giving it, do it with humility and while empowering your loved one. Never give your opinion without first using what I call the three A's. I described them earlier, but they are so important—and so many readers tell me they missed them when reading this book—I list them here again:

Apologize — "Before I tell you what I think about this, I want to apologize because it might feel hurtful or disappointing."

Acknowledge fallibility — "Also, I could be wrong. I don't think I am, but I might be."

Agree to disagree — "And, I hope that we can just agree to disagree on this. I respect your point of view and I will not try and talk you out of it. I hope you can respect mine."

This, too, comes quite easily once you practice it a few times. Try it out with someone in a role-play before using it with your loved one. Practice it in other situations. It will disarm the person you are about to disagree with when you say something like, "I am sorry because my answer might upset you and I realize I could be wrong. I just hope we can agree to disagree. I think _____." Don't use the word "but" as in, "But, I think…" People who are in a disagreement typically stop listening when they hear the word "but."

If your loved one gets defensive after you give your opinion, don't argue. Just apologize for disagreeing. You might even say something like, "I wish I felt differently so we didn't have to argue about this." But I have found that by the time I give my opinion when using LEAP, I rarely encounter defensiveness.

8
Agree

One of the questions I typically get asked when conducting LEAP workshops is, "This sounds great but it must take a lot of time! Who has time to do this?" At this point you may be feeling the same way. In fact, it takes no more time to use LEAP than what you have probably been doing all along. Think of all the time you've wasted arguing or attempting to coerce the person you've been trying to help into accepting treatment. In my experience LEAP does not take more time, and the research I cited earlier on MET confirms that impression. Hopefully, you are now reassured on this count and eager to learn the next step.

Having listened carefully to your loved one's attitudes and feelings about treatment, and having conveyed your empathy, you have undoubtedly found areas where the two of you agree. I never shared Matt's beliefs that God had chosen him as his special messenger to the president, that the CIA was trying to assassinate him, or that he was not ill. But we did agree on at least one thing: that it was very important to keep him out of the hospital. Dolores and I agreed on something similar, and on her goal of getting a job. Although I didn't think it was likely that work was right around the corner for her, I did believe she could start taking some steps in that direction. Vicky and Dr. Kohut agreed to examine together whether she truly needed to take medication after she left the hospital. My brother and I have agreed for a long time now that when he takes his medication regularly he stays out of the hospital, the voices he hears diminish and bother him less, he becomes less fearful, and he is less likely to be asked to leave the coffee houses he likes to frequent.

When you share the same goals, you can
work together instead of being at odds.

iiiiiiiiiiiiiiiiiiiiiiiiiiiiiiiiiiiiiiiiiiiiiiiiiiiiiiiiiiiiiiiiiiiiiiiiiiiiiiiiiiiiiiiiiiiiiiiiiiiiiiiiiiiiiiiiiiiiiiiiiiiiiiiiiiiiiiiiiii

Whenever you see a window of opportunity to convey your observations and opinions, always begin with something your loved one already acknowledges and believes. The more common ground you can find the better. When you share the same goals, you can work together instead of being at odds with one another. Let's look at how to recognize and use a window of opportunity to find common ground.

Recognizing and using windows of opportunity

Dolores believed the main reason she had not been able to find work was because of her frequent hospitalizations. Although this was certainly part of the reason (you can't work and be in the hospital at the same time), it was the end product of what I believed to be more relevant factors. She, however, had very little insight into the more salient reasons she had trouble finding and holding onto a job.

According to her family, Dolores had lost the few jobs she was able to get because of the symptoms of her illness. For example, she would begin talking to herself while at work, having quiet conversations with the voices she was hearing. Sometimes she would become paranoid and accuse her bosses and co-workers of plotting against her.

Dolores, however, didn't recognize the symptoms of her illness, much less the role they played in keeping her unemployed. Instead, she felt her numerous stays in the hospital were causing the problem. Consequently, when we talked about her desire to work, I avoided the issue of symptoms or the role they played in her being fired (unless she specifically asked my opinion about this issue). Instead, I focused on the part of the explanation that we did agree upon—hospitalizations. We agreed that being in the hospital made it impossible for her to work. This led to our agreeing on something else that helped me to formulate a treatment agreement she could accept. But before I tell you more about Dolores, I want to tell you about six things I try to do whenever I see a window of opportunity. When defenses have been lowered and your loved one appears receptive to hearing your views:

1. *Normalize the experience ("I would feel the same were if I was in your shoes.").*

2. *Discuss only perceived problems/symptoms (Statements such as, "I can't sleep at night because I'm constantly on guard. I am so afraid that they're going to come and hurt me," describe insomnia and paranoia stemming from a delusion. However, the words insomnia and delusion never need to be used in your discussions).*

3. *Review perceived advantages and disadvantages of treatment (whether rational or irrational).*

4. *Correct misconceptions (antipsychotic medications are not addictive; serious mental illness is not caused by one's upbringing or use of illicit drugs).*

5. *Reflect back and highlight the perceived benefits ("So if I have it right, you're saying that when you stay on the medication you sleep better and you fight less with your family?").*

6. *Agree to disagree (whenever areas of disagreement are brought to the surface).*

Dolores was angry and frustrated about being hospitalized so frequently and about how this interfered with her goal of getting a job. I empathized with her frustration and anger when I asked, "It sounds like you feel really frustrated about being in the hospital again."

"Very. I need to get out of the hospital and get back to work. I'm going to go crazy if I stay here much longer."

"You're feeling stir crazy?"

"Yes!"

I followed with, "You know something? We're exactly the same that way. I would go absolutely stir-crazy if I were locked up in a hospital and didn't have a job. In fact, I think anyone would feel that way."

With this small bit of self-revelation I was helping to *normalize the experience* Dolores was having. I then asked her if there were any other reasons she was not having luck holding down a job. Some of her ideas made sense, others were illogical, if not frankly delusional, and scattered in between were little kernels of insight into how her disorganized behavior may have contributed to being fired repeatedly.

Noting these instances of insight, I then asked if she wanted my thoughts on *her problem* (notice that we are now talking about a problem *she perceives* she has). She did.

I began by reflecting back what she had said earlier, and then I made a statement in the form of a question, "Well, certainly being in the hospital is interfering with your being able to work. I guess that raises the question of what you can do to stay out of the hospital."

"I don't know. Move away from my family?" she answered wryly.

"Is there any pattern that you've noticed?"

"Well, my father is usually the first one to start picking fights with me. He tells me I'm sick and need to go to the hospital. He's always on my back about taking my medications."

"Why is that?"

"He thinks I'm psycho."

"That bothers you?"

"Yeah, it bothers me."

"I can see why that bothers you. 'Psycho' is a pretty derogatory label to use. Does he actually say that? Does he say you're 'psycho,' or is that how it feels to you?"

"No, he doesn't say it. He thinks I have a chemical imbalance in my brain." Here I am normalizing her experience by acknowledging that being called a psycho would be bothersome, to say the least, to most anyone. It is a derogatory term. I am also asking for clarification.

"So, if you were taking your medications, do you think he wouldn't be on your back?"

"I know he wouldn't."

"I see. And when the two of you fight about the medication, it often ends up with you going to the hospital?"

"I have to, just to get some peace."

"So would it be fair to say that there are two advantages to taking your medications? The first being that your father would not be 'on your back' and the second that you would be less likely to go to the hospital?"

"Yes."

"Yes what?" I asked her to clarify in order to be certain of exactly what it was she was agreeing to.

"If I took my pills my father would leave me alone and I wouldn't have to come here."

"What are some of the *disadvantages* to taking medications?" I followed quickly.

"I am not a psycho, for one. Also, I hate how much weight I gain whenever I'm on them."

"What else? Are there other side effects or other things about the drugs that you see as disadvantages?"

"They make me hear voices. And besides, I don't want to get addicted."

"You are worried about getting addicted?"

"Yes. These are powerful mind-altering drugs."

"They're powerful and they do affect the way you think and feel. Would you like to hear about my experience with the drugs you're taking?"

"You've taken these!?" she asked incredulously.

"Well, not the drugs you're taking now. But over the years I have seen more people than I can count who have taken these medications. My professional experience leads me to the conclusion that the drugs you are taking are *not* addictive and they *don't* cause voices like the ones you hear."

"How do you know?"

"From talking to people who have taken these drugs and from reading the research."

"I always thought they were addictive."

"Well, they're not. At least I've never seen it. Do you still want to put on the list that 'they cause you to hear voices' and they're 'addictive?'"

"No, I guess not."

"Your call," I said, pausing to see if she was going to change her mind. Then I continued. "Any other disadvantages to taking medication?"

"It's embarrassing. I don't want people to know."

"Can we write this down so I can keep track?" I asked, wanting to record while we were together, rather than afterward, the advantages and disadvantages Dolores and I were identifying.

"Sure."

Taking out a pad and pen, I asked, "What were the disadvantages again?"

"They make me feel like I'm psycho, they're embarrassing, and I gain weight."

"And the advantages were what?"

"My father isn't on my back and I stay out of the hospital."

I read the list back to her to make sure I had it right and asked her to keep thinking about the advantages and disadvantages of taking medication.

"Why should I keep thinking about it? You're like everyone else. You want me to take these drugs just like my father," she reacted defensively.

"No, that's not my reason for asking you to keep thinking about it. You have never really asked me my opinion about what I think you should do about taking medications after leaving the hospital. While you are here, I have been clear that I think you should take them. But you haven't asked me what I think you should do afterward. Besides, we weren't really talking about medications. We were talking about your getting a job and how being in the hospital keeps you from your goal."

Dolores visibly relaxed as I spoke and said, "So you don't think I should take the medications after I leave?"

"No, I didn't say that. I said you've never really asked me my opinion."

"So what's your opinion?" I welcomed her question because I felt the time was right to tell her what I thought. She wasn't defensive so I didn't try to delay giving my opinion this time. I said "Well, if we are talking about your goal of getting a job, then I see the same two advantages you see. Your father will be less bothersome and you'll stay out of the hospital. So those are two good reasons to take them. I also see three reasons not to take them. You gain weight, they make you feel like you're a psycho, as you put it, and you feel embarrassed about taking the pills."

"So what's your opinion?"

"I'll tell you if you want, but it might feel disappointing."

"You think I'm psycho!" she said. We both laughed. Before answering, I used the "Three A's": "Look, I'm sorry I feel this way. I don't know everything and I could be wrong. I hope we can agree to disagree about this and be okay. I think you ought to give the medicines a try. You can always change your mind later."

"Why should I?"

"I think, at least in my mind, that the advantages you listed outweigh the disadvantages. Do you agree?"

"I'm not sure," she answered slowly.

"So don't you think it's worth keeping track of? You know, what is good versus what is bad about taking the medications. Because it sounds like when you don't take them it creates a lot of conflict at home and you end up in the hospital."

"I guess so."

"Did I answer your question about what my opinion is about the medication?"

"Yes. You think I should take them if I want my father off my back and I want to stay out of the hospital."

"That's basically right, except you said it would help with your father and ultimately keep you out of the hospital, not me. I said it was important to try and keep track of the pluses and minuses. I also said that I know there are things about taking the medication you don't like." I added this comment to emphasize the fact that I hadn't lost sight of the negatives.

Did you notice how I never once said she should take medication because she has a mental illness?

During another conversation, I had an opportunity to add another benefit to the list we had started. I should mention that I never met with Dolores again without bringing the list we had begun. It was a single piece of paper and at the top I had put a minus sign on the left and a plus sign on the right, with a line down the middle. Advantages were listed under the plus sign and disadvantages under the minus. Prior to the conversation I'm about to recreate, I did a little homework. Luckily, Dolores was on a research unit where we made a point of tracking down and obtaining copies of old medical records. This is something that almost never happens when someone who is seriously mentally ill is hospitalized, although family members and therapists sometimes keep copies, which they then duplicate and give to hospital staff. In any case, I took advantage of the fact that her records were available to look for periods of time when she was hospitalized. Then I compared these instances to times when she was employed. I was not surprised to find that the instances when she was able to work corresponded to the periods when she was regularly taking her medication. So, when we met again I asked Dolores if she wanted to hear what I thought might be another benefit of taking medication. "I think there may be another benefit to taking medication that's not on our list. Want to hear what it is?"

"Okay."

"I was looking over your medical records and discovered an interesting pattern. You were not taking medication almost every time you lost a job. Have you noticed that pattern?"

"No," she answered quickly.

"You answered that kind of fast. Can I suggest something?"

"What?"

"Just think about it some more. Not now. Later. See if you can remember whether you were taking medications when you had a job and whether you and your father were arguing a lot during those times. Can you do that?"

"I can do that. I'll think about it."

"In the meantime, can I add it to our list with a question mark? A possible benefit?"

"Sure. But I don't think it's true."

"Then let's agree to disagree."

"I agree that you're wrong!" she answered with a big grin on her face.

"But you'll keep an open mind about the possibility that I am right, and I'll do the same. I'll stay open to the possibility that you are right. Agreed?"

"Agreed," she answered, serious again.

I don't normally push to put something on the plus side of the list if the person isn't convinced. Usually, I am quick to say we shouldn't list it unless the person is absolutely certain it's a positive. But Dolores liked and trusted me and had a good sense of humor, so I felt more comfortable pushing the issue.

During our subsequent conversations, I tried very hard to follow the six guidelines given above. Whenever possible, I tried to *normalize her experience*, usually by letting her know that if I were in her shoes I would probably feel the same way (about being hospitalized, feeling like my loved ones thought I was a psycho, taking medication). I was very careful to *discuss only those problems (and symptoms) Dolores mentioned herself.* And I took every opportunity I could find to *review the advantages and disadvantages of treatment.* Here as well, I was careful to discuss only the pluses and minuses Dolores had raised herself.

Remember always to ask questions
when you want to make a point

The one time I suggested an advantage she had not identified herself, I first asked if she wanted to hear my opinion ("I think there may be another benefit to taking medication that's not on our list. Want to hear what it is?"). Remember always to ask questions when you want to make a point. By couching your opinion in the form of a question, you emphasize that you want to collaborate and not pontificate. It also gives the person you are trying to convince a sense of control over the conversation. In the end, asking questions usually lowers defenses.

When we spoke, I was constantly on the alert for any misconceptions Dolores held about medication. I *corrected her mistaken belief* that the medications she was taking caused hallucinations and were addictive. Then I asked if she still wanted to put these complaints on the list. If she had said yes, I would have complied, but I would also have asked if we could revisit the issue later.

I *reflected back (repeated) and highlighted the benefits* she mentioned whenever the opportunity presented itself. And we *agreed to disagree* about whether or not Dolores had stopped taking medications prior to losing her jobs.

I encourage you to go back and reread our discussions to see if you can identify when I used each guideline.

||||||||||||||||||||||||||||||||||||||||||||||||||||||||||||||||||||||||||||||||||||||||||||||||||||||||||||||||||||||||||||||||||||||||

From a position of empathy, you can help your loved one to feel more normal and amplify those beliefs that are relevant to arriving at a treatment agreement.

Make and keep a list of the advantages and disadvantages to staying in treatment (drugs, psychotherapy, day programs, occupational therapy, etc.). Be careful always to list any negatives that are mentioned. Doing that both increases your credibility and flags potential obstacles to arriving at a treatment agreement. For example, we have many more medication choices today than we had when my brother first became ill, and the newer medications cause fewer side effects.

Correct misconceptions about treatment whenever you can and highlight any benefits your loved one already experiences. Finally, whenever you come up against an area of disagreement, try and agree to disagree. When you do that you are conveying respect for the other person's opinion, and he will likely be more open to the possibility of being proved wrong. That openness is key to your loved one's reconsidering his position about staying in treatment. Don't be afraid to say that you might also be wrong. If you're not open to being proved wrong, why would you expect your loved one to be?

9
Partner

"How did the psychologist find his wife who was lost in the woods? He followed the psycho-path."
Henry Amador, October 1997

Henry and I agreed that being hospitalized was something to be avoided. We also agreed on his goal of getting a job and obtaining more "pocket money" so he could buy soft drinks, cigarettes, or a hamburger if he felt like it. Although I felt he was much farther away from holding down a job then he did, this difference of opinion was rarely mentioned. Sometimes he would try to corner me by saying, "You don't think I can work right now, do you?" Usually, I was successful in delaying my opinion by saying things like, "I'll tell you what I think if you insist, but what I think doesn't matter. Your opinion is far more important to me, and you think you can. Right?" Usually that was enough to move him from his original question to one that would be more fruitful, such as what it would it take for him to reach his goal.

It took some time, but eventually we agreed that when he took his medication he stayed out of the hospital. At first he attributed the relationship between taking his pills and not being hospitalized to a reduction in the pressure he was getting to stay on the medication rather than any benefit derived from the drugs themselves. In other words, he knew that if he stayed on the medication his doctor and family would not force the issue of hospitalization. In time, however, he came to see his medication as helpful in other ways as well.

Today, if you were to ask him why he takes the medication he would tell you, "It helps me with the voices and it makes me less paranoid." Over the past few years I have noticed that he tells people he has "schizoaffective disorder." I'm not entirely sure if he believes that, but he is light years farther down the path than he was when he first became ill.

His awareness of how medication helps him with *his* problems grew out of the partnerships he developed with various therapists and with me. We often spoke about his fervent desire to get a job. Whenever we did, I empathized with his frustration and encouraged him to try to figure out why he could not keep the jobs he found.

My guess is that he worked in more than a dozen twenty-four hour convenience stores and other odd jobs during the first 10 years of his illness (and hasn't been able to work since).Most stints were for a week at most, ending with his being fired or simply not showing up for work anymore.

He had various explanations to which I listened attentively without challenging their irrationality. Whenever I asked him if I could tell him what I thought, and he said yes, I kept raising the same hypothesis: "Whatever else might be happening," I would tell him, "it's hard to work when you're feeling anxious and hearing voices." Henry knew the medications "blocked the voices" and helped him "feel less paranoid." But he had yet to make the link to how the voices and paranoia interfered with his ability to hold down a job because he was too worried that if he admitted the medications helped him he would be admitting that he was mentally ill. I reassured him, by the way I spoke to him, that this wasn't the case.

Try to agree on goals that are obviously reachable, but don't limit yourself to those.

I can't say for certain how much his gaining the *insight* that finally allowed him to make the connection had to do with his developing the high level of adherence to treatment he currently has. But I am sure it helped the cause, at least a little. I know this because he no longer argues with me as he had in the past – probably because I don't want to argue about such things anymore and also because I couched my opinion as a "hypothesis." I didn't tell him what the problem was. Instead, I gave him my best guess. Instead of being defensive, he listened to my hypothesis and took it in. He was at least considering the possibility that I was correct.

Despite the fact that he has taken his medication more consistently for many years now, he still hasn't reached his goal of holding down a job. This highlights an important point. Try to agree on goals that are reachable, but don't limit yourself to those if you don't have to. Although I thought it would be hard for Henry to work again because he still has some residual symptoms even while on medication, my willingness to talk about his goal gave him hope and a degree of pride. Before that, I used to say, "You're putting the cart before the horse; you have to take medicine and get well before you think about getting a job," which was dismissive and made him feel frustrated with me.

Fortunately, when it came to his goal of obtaining some spending money, I was able to provide him with an opportunity for easy success. Each business day I sent him a check for five dollars, care of his therapist at the day program in which he was enrolled. When I began doing that, I worked out a contract with Henry and his case-worker regarding the things he needed to do in order for the money to be released to him. The main tasks were to attend the program and take his medication. The other requirement was that he not be belligerent and hostile when money was withheld for the days that he missed (for the first several months he missed a day or two every week).

At first Henry felt angry and that I was treating him "like an infant." He felt insulted by my proposal, and I realized that our partnership was in jeopardy of reverting to estrangement. So I stopped and talked with him about his feelings and empathized with his anger and frustration.

I also apologized for having an opinion that differed from his. He felt that if I loved him I should give him the money regardless of whether he went to the day program or not. I could afford it while he had so little money. He was right, I could easily afford this, and he did have very little. Furthermore, he wanted me to send the full amount weekly directly to him, rather than doling it out five dollars at a time and sending it to his therapist. I told him I was sorry but in my view, "and I could be wrong," his attendance at the program was so vital to his getting a job and "doing better" that I wanted to give him an extra incentive to do it. I also said that I worried about what he would do with the money if I sent larger amounts directly to him. Like so many people with serious mental illness, Henry would medicate his illness with alcohol from time to time. After we each heard what the other had to say, Henry felt bribed and I struggled with feeling guilty.

But I stuck to my guns by first apologizing for my position, because I knew it hurt and frustrated him, and explaining, "I really want to help you out. I want to give you this money. But if you are not going to the program, or at least checking in with them everyday, I worry that things are going to go downhill and you'll end up in the hospital again." I added that I thought I might actually make things worse for him if I sent him the money directly. I didn't want to raise the drinking issue just then, so I talked about other concerns I had that were closer to the concerns *he* had.

My brother can be very impulsive with money. He often gives it away to anyone who asks him. This used to happen quite regularly because the people he lived with were, like Henry, on disability insurance and had very little, if any pocket money. He hated saying no but also hated losing the money. So I said, "If we do it my way, when your friends ask you for money, you can honestly say you only have five dollars and you need it." He agreed that this was an advantage to my scheme, although he still wasn't thrilled and didn't think I should have the other concerns I had. He did, however, understand that, right or wrong, these were things that worried me greatly. We ultimately agreed to disagree, but in the process we found something we could agree on. Henry suggested a compromise. Rather than go to the program for the entire day, he would go in the morning to pick up his check, spend a few minutes talking with his caseworker, and take his morning medications in front of her (as you will learn in the next Chapter, I eventually convinced Henry to accept long-acting injectable medication, so this part of our arrangement became much easier). His suggestion immediately made sense to me because I knew my brother found the program tiresome and boring. He felt everyone there was worse off than him. No doubt many of his peers felt the same way. I can't say that I blamed him. I, too, would have found the program he was in at the time excruciatingly boring. I understood his perspective, and he knew it. In the end we agreed that he would go every day to pick up the check and spend a few minutes talking with his caseworker about the previous day. To my surprise, I learned that once he got there he often stayed for several hours.

Our treatment agreement consisted of two main elements: Henry agreed to take his medication (to help him to stay out of the hospital) and go to his day program everyday (so he could have spending money). In the past ten years, he has been hospitalized about six times, always voluntarily, and always for very short stays (usually a few days). I doubt anyone can provide an accurate accounting of the number of hospitalizations he had prior to this period of time. I know for certain he averaged about four hospitalizations per year, each lasting a couple of weeks or longer.

Many other unexpected benefits grew out of our forming a partnership and treatment agreement. Our respect for one another grew, as did our comfort with spending time together. I truly enjoy spending time with him now. He makes me laugh and feel much loved. I think I do the same for him. The picture on the back cover of this book was taken during a visit he made to my house in 1999. He stayed for a week and we had a great time. That picture captures, far better than any words could, how much easier our time together has been these past ten years. He's the one on the right.

Matt

After the hospitalization I told you about in Chapter 4, Matt's parents decided to meet with me so that I could help them to develop the communication skills and techniques I've been describing. As a result, they were able to form a partnership and treatment agreement with Matt similar to the ones I made with Henry. Matt and his parents agreed that it was very important to try to keep him out of the hospital and to reduce the high level of conflict they had at home.

They abandoned the approach of confronting their son with his illness in favor of a more practical and productive approach.

The Blackburns were quick to see the benefits of the approach I taught them. They were tired of fighting with their son and sorely needed a break from all the hostility that had built up between them over the years. They abandoned the approach of confronting Matt with his illness in favor of a more practical and productive approach. They listened and learned that Matt wanted to stay out of the hospital as much as they wanted him to, and he also wished desperately for peace at home. The peace emerged naturally as the Blackburns backed off from trying to convince their son he was ill. It took about two months, but Matt slowly began to listen and to understand how his parents felt about the medication he refused to take.

He felt bad that his mother became very frightened when he was not taking medication. If you recall what Matt was like at home and how he felt about taking medication, this may sound a little far fetched. But Matt's guilt emerged from many discussions with his parents, mostly with his mother, during which they never once told him what he should do. They asked questions, and when he asked them what they thought, they gave their opinion while also acknowledging that they could be wrong. They didn't think it was likely they were wrong about why he needed to take medication, but they could consider the possibility.

When his mother told him he frightened her when he stopped taking medication, Matt felt bad. For this reason, and because his parents said there was a good possibility they might not be able to live with him any longer if he did not take the medicine, Matt agreed that the advantages to taking it far outweighed the disadvantages. This did not happen overnight, but the result was that Matt and his parents accomplished both of the goals they had set out to achieve. I received a card from the Blackburns over the holidays last year. Under Mrs. Blackburn's graceful penmanship conveying the family's good wishes for the New Year her husband had scrawled a little note: "Thanks again for your help. Matt has not been in the hospital in over a year!"

Dolores

Dolores and I agreed on something similar to what the Blackburns had agreed upon, and on her goal of getting a job. Although I didn't think she was going to find a job on Wall Street any time soon I did believe she could start taking some steps in that direction. As I did with my brother, I looked for opportunities to share my hypothesis that she might need to be on medication in order to keep a job. Unlike my brother, but like most people with these illnesses, Dolores was nearly symptom-free when she took her medication. So working full time again in a demanding job was not totally out of the question if she stayed on the medication consistently. As you may recall, I once asked her to keep an open mind about the possibility that medications might make it easier for her to work. At that time she didn't think I was correct, and we *agreed to disagree*. But she did accept my suggestion that she become a scientist and keep an open mind. During her next hospitalization, just five months after the last, we had an opportunity to discuss my theory again. I began by asking her if she had kept the list of advantages and disadvantages to taking medication that we had started when she was in the hospital the last time. She didn't know where it was, but since I had put a copy in her medical record, we were able to go over it again. Her current assessment of the pros and cons to taking medication was consistent with her previous one. When we got to my note about work that was under the advantages column with a question mark, I asked her, "When you were here last you were planning to get a job. Did you have any luck?"

"Yes. I got a job in our local library."

"That's good news. Congratulations. How has it been going?"

"He fired me."

"Who fired you?" I asked.

"The head librarian. He said I talked too much."

"Can I ask you about whether you were taking your medication at the time?"

"No. I stopped. I didn't need it anymore." Showing her the list I had kept, I asked if she remembered why I had put a question mark next to the word "work" in the advantages column.

"We disagreed about that. I was supposed to think about it."

"What do you think?" I couldn't help asking.

"It's true I wasn't taking the medication, but I don't know if that had anything to do with it."

"Okay, shall we make a note of it anyway?" I asked.

"I don't care, sure, go ahead."

"Can you keep an open mind to the possibility that medication helps you to work?"

"Yes," she answered definitively.

Dolores was hospitalized again about three months later, and although she had not found a job in the interim, we talked about the issue again. She was now more open to the idea and admitted that when she stopped taking the medication she talked to herself more. Her family said that one of the problems she had at work was talking to the voices she heard whenever she was off medication. This led to a discussion of how other people might view her talking aloud to herself. She said, "They would think I was nuts!" Having made this link, I tried for another and asked her whether she was hearing voices and talking to herself the last time she was fired. Again, she answered yes.

It took three hospitalizations and encouragement from her family and outpatient psychiatrist, but Dolores finally agreed that taking medication would very likely help her to work. Now everyone was on board with the idea, and her psychiatrist and parents focused on reminding her of this advantage (which she now believed in) rather than trying to get her to understand that she had an illness. The headline here is that Dolores agreed to take her medication even though she still did not think she was ill.

While preparing the revision of this book, I wrote to Dolores to ask how she was doing. She is in her last year of college and has been working in the university library for the past two years. She told me she takes her medicine regularly, that "it doesn't bother" her, and that she is "so used to taking it [she] can't imagine not!"

Vicky

Vicky lowered her medication dosage six months after her hospitalization. As you may recall, she believed that once she was out of the hospital she would no longer need the medicine. She agreed with Dr. Kohut that she would stay on it for at least six months, at which time, if she still wanted to try to go off it, she would do so under her doctor's supervision.

She was seeing Dr. Kohut weekly as they had agreed, and her husband was aware of what she was doing. Dr. Kohut asked Vicky and her husband to keep a daily diary to record their descriptions of her mood, speech, and thinking. They were asked to note if any of the symptoms into which Vicky had insight (grandiosity, euphoria, insomnia, and pressured speech), were returning. After two weeks on a lowered dose of lithium, Vicky reported that she was sleeping less and not feeling tired. She also said that Scott felt she was getting "hyper" and talking more than usual. When I asked her if she agreed with Scott's observation, she reluctantly said yes.

The experiment lasted another two weeks, during which time Vicky became more hyper and started to have grandiose thoughts. Scott asked if he could accompany her to her next session, and she agreed. Vicky admitted to her husband and doctor that she was getting "tired out" again. She was anxious about losing control and asked to have her medication raised again.

No one said anything close to "I told you so," and the question of whether she needed medication for the rest of her life was still on the table. Vicky felt understood and respected by Dr. Kohut and her husband, and she knew that if she wanted to try to go off the drugs again, they would both help her.

I haven't seen her in more than ten years, but I still see Dr. Kohut from time to time. As of this writing, he tells me that Vicky tried one more time to go off her medication but quickly reversed course once the symptoms re-emerged. Since then, her partnership with her husband and doctor has kept her in treatment. Her treatment agreement (that if she wants to go off medication she will do it with the help of her doctor and husband) stands to this day.

Part III

Staying on Guard and Next Steps

"Hope is a good thing - maybe the best thing, and no good thing ever dies."

Stephen King

"Love many things, for therein lies the true strength, and whosoever loves much performs much, and can accomplish much, and what is done in love is done well."

Vincent van Gogh

10

Don't Let Your Guard Down:
The problem of poor adherence

I have, as I've said, used LEAP to convince patients to accept medication on a trial basis even though they continued to believe they were not ill. But I have also learned the hard way always to remember that this person still believes there's nothing wrong with him, and that his belief often leads to his "accidentally," or unconsciously, missing doses. If you also consider the fact that people who are not mentally ill but need to take medication for any number of serious medical problems also have trouble remembering to take their medicine[8], you will see how many doses are likely to be missed.

The problems that arise from such "partial-compliance" can be more subtle, but no less significant, than what happens when someone stops taking his medication completely. For one thing, if everyone (doctor and family) believes the patient is taking his medication regularly and it doesn't appear to be working, they'll assume it's been given a fair trial when that is far from the truth. I've seen many medications written off as ineffective for a particular individual because no one knew the person was missing many, but not all doses. But even if the medicine appears to have some — but not enough — benefit, the doctor may be afraid to raise a high dose even higher when, in fact, the patient is not taking the entire dose that was prescribed in the first place!

---

8. Often, people simply forget to take their medicine. Medication adherence rates in other medical illnesses range from 15 to 50%.

How do I know all this? First, from my experience conducting thousands of interviews using LEAP. I have heard many "confessions" of skipped doses. When someone trusts that you will not scold, criticize, or even comment on such admissions, they feel freer to share them. Add to that the empathy and normalization that follows when you use LEAP (e.g., "I would have skipped the dose too if it were me."), and you are more likely to hear the truth in the future. But research also shows that poor compliance rates (complete and partial nonadherence) averaging between 50 and 75%. Psychiatrists have been found to dramatically overestimate the rate of compliance in their patients. I think they should be forgiven because if their patients were anything like my brother Henry, they are telling their doctors what they want to hear.

The stark fact remains that only 25% of our patients are taking their medication as prescribed. So what can be done to engage such patients in treatment and give them the tools to remember to take their medication—all of it—as prescribed?

11
First Line Treatments

The message light on my answering machine was blinking. I hit the play button and heard, "Xavier, I am calling because Henry missed his appointment for his Prolixin injection today. Please ask him to give me a call to reschedule."[9] It was my brother's case manager, Patricia. Henry and I had met with her after his last hospitalization and agreed that she would be allowed to call me if he missed one of his appointments. It was 1989 and in the past twelve months Henry had not been admitted to the hospital even once, whereas in the past he had been in and out of psychiatric hospitals about four times a year. I believe now, as I did then, that he had done so much better for several reasons — the therapist he was working with, the change in the way I was talking to him (see Chapter 6, Listen), and especially, the way in which he was now getting his medicine.

During his last hospitalization I had lobbied hard to convince Henry to try a long-acting injectable (LAI) medication, rather than taking pills orally, because over the years as a clinician working in hospitals I had seen how much it helped so many others who had also been labeled "revolving-door" patients (or "frequent flyers"). At that time, long acting-injectable, or *depo*, medicines were typically prescribed to individuals being treated involuntarily in

---

9. Long-acting injectable Prolixin (generic name: Fluphenazine Decanoate), is one of three such antipsychotic medicines, all of which last approximately two weeks per injection. The other two are Haldol and Risperdal CONSTA. Haldol and Prolixin are among the older, 1st generation antipsychotic medications and Risperdal is one of the newer, 2nd generation, antipsychotic medications, also called "atypical antipsychotics". Risperdal CONSTA has also been approved by the Federal Drug Administration (FDA) for the treatment of bipolar disorder. One other 2nd generation drug, olanzapine, is likely to be approved by the FDA for use in the United States in the near future.
.

the hospital. The rationale was simple: This person has a history of not believing he is ill and he stops taking his medicine when he leaves the hospital. Consequently, we'll give him something that will last for two weeks at a time. And if he stops taking the medicine (i.e., misses an appointment for the injection), we will know and will be able to reach out to him.

Long-acting injectable medications should be among the first line treatments.

For too long LAI medications have been considered a treatment of last resort. They are offered only after all other avenues have failed. Both the research and my experience tell me that the opposite is true. For patients like my brother, who have long standing problems with insight---and for many others who have difficulty with partial adherence—LAI medications should be among the first line treatments. In other words, they should be among the first medications offered to someone when first diagnosed with a psychotic disorder.

I have seen this strategy work time and again. It's common sense when you think about it. Before Henry agreed to the injections, he would typically promise that if he were released from the hospital he would continue to take his medicine. In fact, he did just what any of us would have done if we believed we'd been wrongfully forced into a hospital and treated for an illness we didn't believe we had. We would tell the doctors and our worried family members what they wanted to hear: "I see now that I am sick and need to take the medicine." It's common sense.

Nevertheless, having to be dishonest with loved ones who are pushing you to take medicine and allying themselves with the psychiatrists who are convinced you are "crazy" is a terrible and lonely predicament to be in.

Before I learned how to listen to my brother, I was angry and felt betrayed whenever he reneged on his promise. But after learning what it was like for him to have to hide pills and lie, after hearing how humiliated and bad he felt about being dishonest, I wanted to find a way to avoid putting him in that predicament again. A simple solution was to lay everything out on the table and not create a situation in which he would be tempted to secretly stop taking the medicine. That is one of several reasons long-acting injectable medication was so helpful to him. All he had to do was show up for an appointment every two weeks and meet with someone he liked. The brief prick of the needle twice a month[10] was far less difficult for him than having to struggle three times a day with the conflict between loyalty to his family and his desire to stop taking the medicine. He wanted to please our mother and me because he knew how worried we were about him, but because his illness had convinced him nothing was wrong, he found himself caught between a rock and a hard place more than 90 times a month! Now it was just twice a month, and we all knew whenever the conflict got the best of him and the "denial" won out.

Another, similar case with which I am personally familiar involved Millie, who is the mother of Tina and Susan and the subject of Susan's documentary film "Out of the Shadow" (see Resources section at the back of this book). I was the consultant for the film and am also a family friend. Like my brother, Millie has a long history of schizophrenia and of hiding the fact that she is not taking her medicine. Once, while flying on an airplane on her way to visit Susan, Millie went into the bathroom, poured out the contents of every one of her capsules of antipsychotic medication, then put the empty capsules back together and into the bottle. She did this because she knew her daughter would

---

10. New formulations of 2nd generation LAI's have been developed that need to be given only once a month.

be checking to see if she was swallowing the pills. I can't blame Millie for what she did. She didn't think she was ill. I wouldn't want to take medicine for an illness I didn't believe I had! Would you? I would probably do the same thing if I were in her shoes.

As the film shows, when Millie is taking her medication, she does wonderfully, but she relapses whenever she is able to avoid taking the medicine. It was during her last relapse, when Susan and Tina were talking together with me about Millie's treatment options, that I strongly encouraged them to get her on Risperdal CONSTA. She had previously done well on atypical medications, and I felt that a long-acting injectable would give Millie the best chance of staying well and recovering more fully. At that time, and as of this writing, CONSTA was the only atypical antipsychotic available in a long-acting injectable form. Susan and Tina were able to use their positive relationship with their mother to convince her to accept twice-monthly injections, and, not surprisingly, to my knowledge since she has been on this form of medication there has not been another relapse. Among other positive benefits, Millie is no longer tempted to secretly stop taking her pills. Like my brother, Millie is now on a steady dose of medication and unable to act on her natural ambivalence without her doctor and family knowing about it.

Medication: Which one and how it's given

Very often when I'm giving a LEAP seminar someone wants to know, "What medication is best?" The answer is "none." My experience and the science agree that we cannot reliably predict which medication will be best for any particular individual. When deciding on a specific medication one needs to balance, among other things, how well it is working against the side effects for that individual. In some instances cost is also a deciding factor.

That said, however, I do believe that certain generalizations can be made when it comes to choosing medications for people with a history of poor insight and poor adherence to medication. In short, keep the dosing simple and make it hard for the person to succumb to his desire to stop taking the medicine.

My advice is to keep it simple if you can.

When a medication is taken once or twice a day as compared to several times a day or more, it is far easier to monitor the patient's adherence. And it is also easier for the person taking the medicine to remember and not succumb to an unconscious desire to skip a dose. The fewer doses per day, the fewer opportunities the person will have to consciously or unconsciously decide to skip a dose *or simply to forget.*

When patients of mine have a history of poor insight and poor adherence to medication, I often recommend a long-acting injectable drug.

When patients of mine have a history of poor insight and poor adherence (i.e., partial or complete non-compliance) to medication, I often recommend a long-acting injectable drug. Not only does this make it easier for the patient and easier for me to monitor his compliance, but it does away with other issues as well. For example, the person administering the dose doesn't have to ask the patient to open his mouth to prove he swallowed the pills (I would be thrilled if I never had to do that again) or secretly count how many pills are left in the bottle to try and get a read on whether or not he is taking all his medicine

But once again, you don't not have to take my word for it (nor would I want you to). There is research that supports what I've learned from personal experience. For example, in 1999 Young and his colleagues published a comprehensive review of research studies (see literature cited at the back of this book) that found that, on average, about 50% of the patients who were taking pills stopped taking their medication as compared to only 17%, of those who were receiving long-acting injections. This essential finding has been replicated numerous times.if you decide to go this route, don't be scared off by the prospect of trying to convince someone to take a shot twice a month. It's not as difficult as you might think. In fact, I have been involved in some research on this issue[11] and found that if you use the main elements of LEAP you are likely to be successful. But whether or not you can convince the person you are trying to help to take a long-acting injectable medication, remember to simplify the dosing, closely monitor that the medicine is *actually being taken*, and never stop listening to how your patient or loved one experiences taking medicine.

As a final comment on the subject of medication, I'd like to speak to a question I'm frequently asked: "If anosognosia is a symptom of mental illness, like flat affect or hallucinations, can medicines help?" As I've already said, few studies have examined this question specifically. Generally, anosognosia, like other negative symptoms, appears to be resistant to drug treatment. Although there are two studies in the literature that suggest that Clozaril and Risperdal Consta may improve insight,[12]it's important to remember what I've noted about the importance of replication (i.e., Aristotle's observation that "one swallow does not make a summer"). Although promising, these studies must be independently replicated before we can know if the findings are valid.

11. Lasser R, Gharabawi GM, Jarboe K, Litrell K, Miller AL, M.D., Amador XF, Weiden PJ,Schooler NR, Docherty JP, and Crumbley E. (2005). Patient Acceptance and Long-Acting Risperidone: the Start Program and Gain Approach. Presentation at the annual meeting of the American Psychiatric Association.

12. Pallanti S, Quercioli L, Pazzagli A (1999), Effects of clozapine on awareness of illness and cognition in schizophrenia. Psychiatry Res 86(3):239-249.

Gharabawi GM, Lasser RA,Bossie CA, Zhu Y, Ballenger JC and Amador XFA. Insight and Its Relationship to Clinical Outcomes in Patients with Schizophrenia or Schizoaffective Disorder Receiving Long-acting Risperidone. Journal of International Clinical Psychopharmacology. (in press)

Psychotherapy

Does psychotherapy do anything for people with serious mental illness? If you've read this far, you now know why I believe it does. Many people have asked me for referrals to therapists who use LEAP. Others have asked me for advice about how to convince a therapist who is not trained in LEAP to try this method.

Since the first edition of this book was published in the summer of 2000, thousands of therapists and family members have been trained in LEAP. LEAP is as much a communication style as it is a form of therapy, and because it is intuitive and helps very quickly, most therapists are willing to learn it once they get a feel for it.

Many therapists already use some elements of LEAP,
but not as systematically as they should and without
understanding its full potential.

It has been my experience that many therapists already use some elements of LEAP, but not as systematically as they should and without understanding its full potential. When I point out the specific instances when they have used reflective listening, which is the cornerstone of this method of communicating with patients, they quickly acknowledge that it reduces tension and distrust and opens lines of honest communication about symptoms and treatment. At its best, it helps patients find reasons to be in treatment that make sense to them and transforms the LEAP practitioner from a potential adversary into someone patients trust and whose opinion they value. For these reasons, I find that once they get a taste of it, most therapists are not only open but also eager to learn more about this way of working.

Many therapists have been trained in LEAP through LEAP Institute (see www. LEAPInstitute.org). This year is the first year we have begun to compile a list of certified therapist, however, thousands of others have attended LEAP trainings over the past decade that we have not kept track of. So if you cannot find a certified LEAP trained therapist in your community, there are some questions you can ask to find out if the therapist you are dealing with, or considering, has attended one of our earlier seminars and is using the core LEAP tools. For example, you can ask if he or she has ever attended a LEAP seminar or training day or read this book. You can ask if he or she has received any training in Motivational Interviewing. If the answer is "no," you can then ask if he or she would be willing to read this book (loan them your copy).

How to Convince a Therapist to Read This Book

While it's somewhat embarrassing for me to offer this next bit of advice and I run the risk of offending my fellow-therapists, I do it because I've been told countless times by readers who are family members that, "We gave a copy of your book to our loved one's therapist, but we don't think he's read it! How do we get him to read it?" I have contemplated this question, wondering what I would do if I were that therapist. And then I remembered that on occasion I have, indeed, been given books by patients and family members. One of the things that usually got me to crack the book's spine was a request for my opinion. Questions like, "I thought this book was helpful and I'd like to work this way, what do you think? Should I?" usually got me to read at least the first chapter and skim the rest. You could try questions such as, "Our family has been working this way with our loved one and we wanted to make sure we weren't interfering with anything you're doing. Could you have a quick look and let us know?"

Don't be discouraged if you encounter some initial resistance. Remember that it took me seven years of arguing with my brother before I started to work this way! And, in fact, most therapists got into the business because they have a genuine desire to be helpful.

Cognitive Therapy

Finally, cognitive therapy has proved to be effective for reducing the severity of certain symptoms in patients with psychotic disorders (see Chapter on Psychotherapy for Psychotic Disorders). As I mentioned earlier, the fact that we are dealing with disorders of the brain means that we need to attack the deficits with both biological and psychological treatments, just as we do when someone has a stroke or some other form of brain dysfunction. Despite being effective for many patients, however, cognitive therapy is still underutilized in the treatment of psychotic disorders in the U.S. whereas in other countries such as the United Kingdom it is more widely available. Nevertheless, its use is growing. I devote a chapter to this topic and at the end of this book I provide you with recommended readings and an organizational resource so that you can learn more about this important tool for the treatment of psychosis.

Having said all this, however, there are times when we can't wait for LEAP or other forms of psychotherapy to take effect. If someone is off medication and in crisis we may need to step in and take over. Doing that is rarely easy, and in the next three chapters I'll be helping you to recognize when it's time to seek involuntary treatment and how to go about it. But just as importantly, I'll also be explaining how you can use LEAP to preserve your relationship with your loved one even when you need to take these drastic measures.

12
Involuntary Treatment

When I give lectures and workshops on LEAP I am often applauded as someone who has helped both those who would like to see more options for involuntary treatment and those who would like to have such laws revoked. The first edition of *I am Not Sick, I Don't Need Help!* has been used by some people to argue that less intrusive measures, including LEAP, are available and should be used in place of involuntary treatment and by others who point to the research on anosognosia to argue that involuntary treatment is the humane thing to do when someone refuses treatment because of poor insight. So where do I stand on this issue? We need these laws. But when or whether they should be invoked depends on individual circumstances.

I have personally been involved in initiating more involuntary treatments than I can count. I have no doubt that my participation in such treatments not only saved lives but also helped my patients avoid injury or being arrested and charged with a crime.Certainly these interventions gave many a shot at recovery from mental illness. But for me, involuntary treatment is often the last resort. For all those it has helped, I know that many times it was traumatic for the person with mental illness and, for many, nothing more than a band-aid (unless the ordered treatment was continued on an outpatient basis). Over the years I have learned a lot about when and how to pursue this option and how to optimize the outcome. It does not have to be a traumatic experience for your loved one or for you. In this chapter I will talk about those instances when I believe forcing treatment is necessary, the options available to you, and some advice on how to do it.

---

*Certain situations are a "no-brainer" and
almost always warrant commitment.*

In Chapter 1 I described how Matt's mother called the police when Matt became threatening during an argument because she knew from past experience that he was losing control of his temper and would likely become violent. Having survived many episodes of her son's illness, she knew when it was time to call for help. On the face of it, the signs of illness to which Matt's mother was alert were different from those I learned to watch for in my brother Henry. But the degree of danger they signaled was very similar. The signs for which you need to learn to watch may also be unique. But whenever a person is acting in a threatening or dangerous manner either *verbally* (e.g., "Stop transmitting waves at me or I will make you stop!" or more blatantly (e.g., "I am going to hit you if..." or "I am going to kill you...") or *physically* (e.g., throwing things, pushing or restraining another person, lighting a fire in a waste basket, picking up a bat or knife, locking you out of the house or locking you in a room, etc.) you have to act. The same holds true if the person is expressing any ideas about ending his own life. Certain situations are "no-brainers" and almost always warrant commitment. Obvious among these are those situations in which someone is obviously about to hurt himself or someone else. In fact, being harmful to oneself or others is the most common legal standard for committing someone to a hospital against his will.

---

*If you are the doctor or therapist, it is almost
always good practice to contact the family to
share your observations and concerns.*

If you have decided to act, remember that you are not the first person who has had to commit a mentally ill person and there are many resources available to you. If you're are a family member, the first person to contact when you feel the situation is spiraling out of control is the therapist or doctor who has been working with your loved one (if he or she is seeing someone). If he has not seen a therapist or doctor in a long time, or has never seen a mental health professional, the first person you contact will have to be someone different, and I will get to that shortly.

If you are a doctor or therapist, it is almost always good practice to contact the family to share your observations and concerns. Hopefully, you have been working as a team up to this point. But even if you haven't, it's never too late to join forces. For many therapists, this advice goes against their training and ethics. What is said in therapy is supposed to stay in the room, with very few exceptions. But—although most therapists are not currently trained this way—an exacerbation of a serious mental illness (e.g., psychotic decompensation) is good cause to breach confidentiality so that you can speak with others who care about your patient. If the limits of confidentiality are clear up front ("If you become sick and it affects your good judgment, I will need to inform your family to get their help."), there is no ethical dilemma. I have done this many times and have never been sued or received complaints. More important, it is the right thing to do.

There are generally three ways to start the ball rolling. So far, I have only mentioned calling the police. In fact, there are other options I almost always consider first unless I feel someone is clearly in immediate danger of harming himself or someone else. Ideally, my order of preference is to: 1) Go together to the E.R.; 2) Call a mental health crisis team or an assertive community treatment team; or, if all else fails, 3) Call the police and ask for officers from the department's Crisis Intervention Team (CIT).[13]

My order of preference is to:

1. *Go together to the E.R.*
2. *Call a mental health crisis team or assertive community treatment team*
3. *Call the police and ask for officers from the department's Crisis Intervention Team (CIT)*

Use your LEAP skills to make this happen

Sometimes, if your relationship is one in which the person still trusts you, you can ask him to go to the E.R. with you. Explain that you're worried about him and want to see if the doctor can help. Use your LEAP skills to make this happen. And be sure to focus on what the person believes the problem to be. Once, when Henry was very ill and paranoid about our mother, believing she would kill him, I said, "You need to get away from Mom right now. Let's go for a ride and drop by Kino [the county hospital] so you can feel safer." He agreed. One mother convinced her mentally ill daughter to go to the hospital with her after they had talked about the daughter's suicidal feelings. The mother, after doing reflective listening and normalizing her daughter's feelings about wanting to die, then asked, "Can I tell you what I would do if I were you?"

"What do you think I should do?"

"I think we should go together and talk to a doctor just in case that helps. And if you still feel this way afterwards, then you haven't really lost anything."

"But they'll lock me up if I go."

---

13. CIT is another fast growing innovative and effective approach to helping persons with mental illness. For more information please see: (http://www.citinternational. org/) and also (http://www.nami.org/Template.cfm?Section=CIT2)

"They might. But even if they do, you don't have anything to lose. If you still feel this way later, at least you will know that you tried." By using reflective listening and not lying about what was likely to happen, she was able to convince her daughter to go to the hospital.

You may be tempted, but try hard not to trick the person by telling him you are going someplace else and then ending up at the E.R.. I know many people who have tried this trick, and I did it myself once, but it's risky for two reasons: The person will justifiably feel betrayed and/or might jump out of the car when he realizes where you are really going. It can work, but I don't recommend it over the other options I recommend.

To find out if your community has a crisis team, you can call any psychiatric emergency room or your local police department.

Many police departments and psychiatric emergency rooms work in partnership to keep mentally ill people who commit minor offenses (such as disturbing the peace) out of jail. A common product of this partnership is the "mobile crisis team" (a.k.a. crisis team; mobile acute crisis team; psychiatric crisis unit, etc.). Usually, mobile crisis teams are based in mental health agencies or hospitals. To find out if your community has a crisis team, you can call any psychiatric emergency room or your local police department.

The way this type of intervention works is that the mental health workers come to your loved one and evaluate him on the spot. If they judge that hospitalization is warranted, they will try to convince your loved one to accompany them to the hospital. If he refuses, they can initiate the commitment process immediately. Because they're trained to recognize mental illness, they're less apt than the police to misinterpret your loved one's behavior as something else (e.g., criminal behavior, the result of a negative character trait, etc.). They may also be able to communicate with your loved one more effectively than the average police officer who has not received the same specialized training. If no mobile crisis team exists, or none is unavailable when you call, then contact your local police. When you do, explain that your loved one is mentally ill and in imminent danger of hurting himself or someone else (if applicable).

You may naturally be resistant to the idea of calling the police because you feel that by having your loved one committed you are trying to take control of his life. And, if you are already struggling with a tenuous or strained relationship, it is only natural to want to avoid the conflict such a move will create. This avoidance and the desire to not be hurtful often lead to procrastination and second thoughts. This is normal but potentially dangerous for all the reasons I discussed in Chapter 2 (i.e., poor response to treatment when left untreated for years, poorer course of illness, suicide, risk of violence, etc.). It is also dangerous because so many people with untreated mental illness are ending up in our jails and prisons. This is not a good solution. Our jails and prisons are notorious for providing inadequate mental health treatment. There are exceptions to this rule, but not many. Worse, the individual who has been charged and jailed usually ends up with a criminal record that will forever change the course of his life. In tens of thousands of cases such persons lose a lot more than 72 hours (the typical involuntary treatment hold) of their freedom. If you initiate an involuntary treatment the chances of this happening are far less than when a complete stranger is the triggering cause. But to succeed, it is imperative for you to believe that commitment is not a permanent violation of your loved one's autonomy. In fact, in most cases it is a means by which you can help your loved one *regain* control of his life and self-determination. That is why resolving your ambivalence and guilt early on is vital to the commitment process.

Resolving your ambivalence and guilt

As right as you think your decision is, it's difficult not to feel guilty sometimes and to falter in your resolve. The term "commitment" conjures up images of physical struggle and straightjackets. When we think of a psychiatric ward, the picture of a nurturing and stabilizing environment is generally not the one that comes to mind. Images from the movie *One Flew Over the Cuckoo's Nest* are far more common.

Like most people, I initially had a very negative image of psychiatric institutions. I wrote in my preface to the first edition of this book:

"Having never stepped foot inside a psychiatric ward, I felt nervous and self-conscious. Nervous for the same reasons most people are made uneasy when surrounded by twenty or so people with serious mental illness. Some of them were pacing and talking aloud to the voices they alone heard. Others were passionately smoking cigarettes. One man sat quietly, directly in front of me, his eyes fixed on some far away vision. Was I safe? Were they safe? Was this a hell-hole or a haven? These were just a few of the anxious questions running through my mind...I was sure I would somehow be blamed for what had happened to my brother... for the police, the ambulance, and the restraints he had endured because of me."

In fact, after my brother was committed the first time, I learned that the ward he went to was nothing like what I imagined in my worst fears. Yes, there was a lot of smoking (although even that is now a thing of the past in most hospitals), but no one was sitting around in straightjackets screaming. None of the patients were threatening or bothered me in any way. Henry had been restrained, but that had been only briefly and in the ambulance. When he got to the E.R. they soon released him from the lambskin-lined cuffs. The ward he was on, like many I have worked in, had a day room, or lounge, with a television playing softly in one corner. There was a ping-pong table on the other side of the room. I was able to visit my brother and spend time with him in that room. The reality of the ward quickly allayed my worst fears. The truth is that most in-patient treatment facilities are designed to be comfortable, humane, and reassuring to the people who are being treated there.

In order to effectively help your loved one, it is necessary to either work through, or temporarily put aside, the fears and doubts you have about commitment. The most important thing you need to do is try to separate myth from reality. Learn about the commitment process and what the facilities in your area are like. Many of the consumer-based (or patient-based) organizations described in the Resources section of this book can help you to learn what you can expect from your local mental health facilities.

This advice is relevant for some mental health professionals as well. So many times, those of us who work primarily in outpatient settings hesitate to commit patients because of a fear of facilities with which we are not intimately familiar.

Serious mental illness is like any other medical illness.

Serious mental illness is like any other medical illness. If your loved one had diabetes, you would learn everything you could about the illness and what steps to take to control the disease. You would try to locate the best centers for the treatment of diabetes in your area. You would have emergency medical numbers by the phone and know the closest emergency facility in case anything unexpected happened. If the diabetes flared up and your loved one became confused and disoriented, you would not hesitate to pursue hospitalization, whether your loved one wanted it or not. And I am fairly certain that you would not feel guilty or ambivalent.

Recognize the warning signs.

If you have gone through previous hospitalizations with your loved one, you are probably familiar with the early warning signs that signal the need for hospitalization. You know when your loved one is acting out of character and the illness has worsened.. Take a moment to stop and write down the three most worrisome changes in your loved one's thinking, perceptions, and/or actions that you feel warranted hospitalization in the past (or that you think should warrant it).

1.

2.

3.

Keep your list in mind and refer to it often. If you are mindful of the early warning signs, you will be less likely to get caught off guard when the illness flares up. Here are some common signs that others have considered serious enough for them to contemplate commitment:

- *Refuses to take medication when the family and therapist know from past experience that deterioration and harm are imminent*
- *Verbally or physically abusive*
- *Suicidal ideas (e.g., "I wish I was dead," "I should just end it all," etc.)*

- *Harms self (e.g., cuts body parts, bangs head, drinks soap, eats dirt, etc.)*
- *Is destructive of property (own or others)*
- *Stalks others (e.g., incessant phone calls despite complaints, repeated unwanted visits, etc.)*
- *Homeless, resulting in harm to self (e.g., exposure to extreme weather conditions without appropriate clothing, poor nutrition, neglect of essential health care, etc.)*
- *Refuses or is unable to speak with anyone*
- *Delusions of grandeur (e.g., has superhuman powers, is famous, knows famous people personally, etc.)*
- *Talks to self excessively*
- *Speech is unintelligible*
- *Delusions of persecution (e.g., being watched by government agents, possessed by the devil, fears loved ones intend harm, etc.)*
- *Command hallucinations (e.g., voices that say "you must kill yourself," etc.)*
- *Significant deterioration in self-care and hygiene*
- *Dangerous due to disorganization (e.g., starts fires unintentionally by dropping lit cigarettes, etc.)*
- *Inadequate care of dependants (e.g., neglect, isolates children or the elderly from other family members, etc.)*
- *Poor judgment (e.g., uncharacteristically sexually provocative and/or promiscuous, stops paying bills, wild spending sprees, gives away all possessions, loses job due to "eccentric" behavior, fails to keep appointments, or fails to follow procedures necessary to receive benefits)*
- *Health is deteriorating (e.g., self starvation, refuses to seek medical help for other serious illnesses, mixes prescribed medications with illicit drugs, etc.)*

These examples may or may not be relevant to your situation. I list them for two reasons: to give you an idea of what others have found to be important signs and to remind you that you are not the only person who has had to make this decision. In the Resources section you will find a list of organizations that can put you in touch with people who have had first hand experience dealing with commitments (e.g., *www.nami.org*, *www.psychlaws. org*, and others).

There are less immediate methods: the civil commitment hearing and court-ordered assisted outpatient treatment.

In addition to the three avenues just described, there are several less immediate methods: the civil commitment hearing, guardianship, advance directives (where the person with mental illness, when doing well, has legally designated someone to take charge of his treatment should he become ill again), and court-ordered assisted outpatient treatment (AOT). Since the first edition of this book was published, more options for AOT have been created in a number of states across America. Although inpatient involuntary treatment typically requires that the mental illness make the person a danger to self or others, persons with chronic psychotic disorders who show certain patterns of behavior as a consequence of their illness may receive court-ordered treatment on an outpatient basis. To find out if your state has such a law and how to use it, I encourage you to go to the Treatment Advocacy Center's website www.PsychLaws.org. There, you will also find information on guardianship, advance directives, and other options.

The Treatment Advocacy Center is funded by the Stanley Research Foundation and was founded by psychiatrist E. Fuller Torrey and others who were concerned about the millions of mentally ill Americans who were refusing treatment because of anosognosia (poor insight) and suffering terribly as a result. Remember Michael Kass, from Chapter 4, the patient I met in the E.R.? He had been found hiding in a subway train tunnel. When the police found him, he hadn't eaten or bathed in several days and he had made camp dangerously close to an active track, explaining that "they [federal agents] would never think to look for me here." Michael had a history of responding well to medication. When he was on medicine he was able to care for himself and did not do things that put his life in danger. But because he didn't see that he was ill, he always stopped taking the medicine the moment he was discharged from the hospital, thus starting the cycle all over again. Michael is one of the many people who have benefited from AOT.

He understood that I believed I was helping him,
even though he didn't agree that he needed help.

When you commit someone to a hospital you may feel that you have created an irreparable breach of trust. But when it's done from a position of love and support, it is almost always perceived as a gift. From my personal experience with my brother, I know that although it took about four hospitalizations, Henry eventually came to see my interventions into his life (calling the police and his psychiatrists) as expressions of my love for him. He understood that I believed I was helping him, even though he didn't agree that he needed help. This was a great source of consolation for both of us during the next several years it took for him to realize that he was in need of treatment (i.e., for us to agree).

In this chapter we've talked about how to determine whether and when to commit. Since you chose to read it, the answer may be that the time to commit is now. If, after using the techniques I've offered and your loved one is still refusing treatment, you have probably begun to seriously consider commitment as an option. If your loved one is seriously ill and not getting treatment, he or she needs help now. Remember that if this same person were suffering from a flare-up of some other medical condition like diabetes or had been in an accident, you would not hesitate to corral him into the car and take him to the hospital no matter how much he protested. Sooner or later, even if he still believes he is not sick, if you can help him to recognize that what you did was done out of love, he will most likely be grateful.

13
How to Do It

I was 21 years old and deciding on a career in psychology when schizophrenia exploded in Henry's brain like some impossibly patient time-bomb planted by his genes. Suddenly, only a day after our stepfather's death, Henry was talking about hearing voices and having "crazy" thoughts that couldn't possibly be true. He was 29 at the time, but had been slowly becoming odd and isolated since his mid-twenties.

The night our stepfather died of a heart attack, it was Henry who found him on the high school track where Dad had gone jogging. I was the first one Henry called with the news. I called my older brothers and sisters who lived scattered across the country and left that same night for Arizona, where Henry was living with our parents. The next morning, Henry met me at the airport.

During the half-hour drive across town in his bright-blue, 52 Chevy pickup. I struggled with feeling embarrassed whenever we had to stop at a red light, but not because of the thirty-year-old truck painted the color of a turquoise Caribbean sea. True, the color was strange even for Tucson in the early eighties and caused a few stoplight stares, but Henry's choice of color didn't embarrass me. As far as I was concerned, Henry could paint that truck any color under the sun after all the blood and sweat he poured into its resurrection. Damned thing could have been pink, and I would still think of Henry as a model of masculinity. He must have rebuilt motors on a dozen cars in his day. No, I could never be embarrassed by his bright-blue pick-up. It was the talking to himself that made me wonder what we must have looked like to other drivers. Henry wasn't looking at me. Maybe he couldn't?

Mostly he stared straight ahead, talking and laughing to himself. Sometimes, he would turn to look out his open window at the car next to us and just keep on talking nonsense to the passenger in the adjacent car. At every stoplight I saw perplexed and fearful expressions, a window rolled up, at one, "the finger."

Green lights offered some relief from the tension that was building inside me; no one would notice now, and it was just the two of us. Or was it? Henry kept right on talking and mumbling to himself as if I weren't there, almost as if he were having a conversation with someone I couldn't see. When I first asked him what he was saying, he laughed and said, "Ohh, Javi my little brother, he's here, ha ha ha." Then, abruptly becoming serious, "Dad had an accident. Oh, no, no, no. I was playing the guitar when I killed him, the music got in his head and he tripped and fell, he was too, he mmmhuh bad Papi his soul you know? His bow-toe-blow you know?" His speech kept dissolving like that into unintelligible syllables and nonsensical rhymes mumbled over an occasional phrase. Mostly word salad, with fragments of coherent thoughts – disturbing thoughts. After a few more attempts at rational conversation, I gave up. I was still processing the news he had given me over the phone the night before. As odd as my brother sounded, *I was playing the guitar when I killed him,* I was mostly thinking of my mother, who had just lost her second husband, and about myself. I was not yet concerned about what was happening to Henry.

By the time Henry and I arrived at my parents' house, now my mother's house, I had successfully tuned him out. But over the course of that longest day of my young life, it became clear to me that he was very seriously sick. He was psychotic. Maybe even schizophrenic. Most people, including my family at the time, don't know what that means. But I did. I was a senior in college studying psychology and I recognized the symptoms, among them hearing voices and delusions. And so by the end of that week, because I was the "family psychologist" and also the one closest to Henry, I was elected – given the task of getting Henry into the hospital, or, more to the point, away from the rest of us who were grieving and reeling from our stepfather's unexpected death at the age of fifty-eight. We had a funeral to plan, a loved one to bury, and no interest in dealing with Henry's mental illness.

At first I tried to convince him he was sick and needed help, and as you well know, utterly failed. Unfortunately, being new to all this, I immediately jumped to trying to get him involuntarily committed. But the psychiatrist in the E.R. with whom I spoke wasn't having it. He asked me, "Is he threatening anyone?"

"No," I answered truthfully.

"Is he threatening to kill himself?"

"No."

"Then there's nothing I can do. Call back if he becomes a danger to himself or others."

Henry and I went round and round that week, but when I went back to New York he was still in the throes of his first psychotic episode. About a month later, after the rest of the family had cleared out, I received the first of many such phone calls from my mother. "You need to come here quick. Henry is not in his right mind. He needs to be in the hospital."

I returned to Arizona, and this time I was more successful. Henry had been talking about suicide. I called the police, told them he was mentally ill and suicidal, and they took him to the hospital. He was back in three hours! He was angry, hurt, and felt betrayed. "How could you call the police on your own brother? Did I steal from you? Did I try and hurt you?!" Worse than that he felt vindicated. "See! There's nothing wrong with me. Even the psychiatrist said so!"

Actually, what had happened is that Henry quickly figured out that his talking about feeling suicidal was what had triggered the police taking him into custody. He realized that as long as he didn't talk about it, he would not be admitted to the hospital. And he was right.

As we talked long into that night, I realized I had to try again. Without telling Henry what I was going to do, I called the police the very next night. I told them he was mentally ill and threatening suicide. He was also drinking too much, but I didn't add this fact. When they arrived, I stayed locked up in the bedroom with my mother so that Henry would have to answer the door. That was one of many mistakes I made that night. Fortunately, Henry went quietly, but the damage I did to our relationship took a long time to heal.

Although I was mostly well intentioned, I made many mistakes I now wish I hadn't. Some of what I did was positive, like talking to the psychiatrist after Henry was released the first time I tried to get him hospitalized. But still, I made some serious mistakes that will be instructive to talk about here.

What I should have done

The first mistake I made was not encouraging Henry to talk with his therapist. He had seen a therapist the year before, for depression, and although I knew that, I did not try to utilize their existing relationship. I knew Henry liked Roy, and I should have called him for advice. Ideally, I could have suggested to Henry that he meet with Roy to talk about Dad's passing and just dropped the whole "you're mentally ill and need to go to the hospital" issue. But I wasn't thinking about Henry's perspective yet. I was being the family shrink.

After deciding to go the route of an involuntary admission to the hospital, I should first have checked to see if there was a crisis team, staffed by mental health professionals, that could come out to the house and evaluate my brother.

Instead, I went straight to 911. Before I go further, I want to be very clear that I am not being hard on myself. I was new to all this. You should not be hard on yourself either. The only time I feel deeply guilty about my relationship with Henry is when I don't learn from my mistakes.

The most obvious, and frankly frightening mistake I made was letting Henry answer the door when the police came that second time. He was psychotic. He was paranoid. Although more and more police are now being trained to deal with mentally ill people, back then it was very rare. A terrible tragedy could have unfolded that night if Henry had become frightened and began speaking delusionally and in a threatening manner to the officers. Had they felt they were in danger, they would have ordered him to the ground, and he, very likely, would not have been able to comply because he was so disorganized and barely in touch with reality.

Instead, I should have met the officers outside and explained that my brother was mentally ill, had no criminal history, and was not threatening to hurt anyone but himself. By saying these things I would have made it clear that they were going to meet someone who was loved and that I was asking them to take great care. But I did neither of those things, and I was very lucky that night.

Finally, I should have telephoned the psychiatrist when Henry arrived at the ER so that Henry wouldn't again deny being suicidal and so be released. Better yet, I should have gone down in person. But again I was lucky, because Henry was so upset about opening the door to find several police officers wanting to "arrest" him that, when he spoke to the psychiatrist, he apparently didn't think to hide the fact that he had been feeling suicidal.

The system is set up to put a wall between mental health professionals and their patients' families

Once Henry was admitted to the hospital, I made the very common mistake I talked about in Chapter 2. Exhausted by the whole experience, I took a break and did not stay involved. Although I went to a family meeting and visited my brother (he refused to speak to me during these visits), I did not attempt to stay in touch with his treatment team or participate in the discharge plan. Part of the reason was naiveté on my part and part of the reason is that the system is set up to put a wall between mental health professionals and their patients' families.

One of the most important things a family member can do is to stay active and in touch with their loved one's mental health care providers. This is true whether your loved one is in the hospital or an outpatient seeing his therapist once every several weeks or more. During our one meeting with Henry's doctor and social worker, my mother and I should have asked about the discharge plan and shared our observations about what we thought would and would not work. The most important observation we could have shared is that Henry did not think he was sick. We should have held the professionals accountable with the question: "Given that he does not believe he's ill, what good will your prescription and outpatient appointment slip do?"

Henry agreed to renew his relationship with Roy, his previous therapist. But once again, I did not attempt to open a line of active communication with the therapist. For example, I did not ask Henry if I could go to his first session to explain my view of the events that had led to his hospitalization. Within days of leaving the hospital Henry had stopped taking the medicine, and within weeks he apparently stopped going to see Roy. I wasn't sure about the latter because I was not communicating with Roy and had to rely solely on what Henry told me. In his defense, at that time my brother mostly wanted me to stop intruding on his life and telling him he was sick. Giving me permission to talk to his therapist was probably not going to be high on his list of priorities. But the point is, at that time, I never tried.

I did eventually try, and I encountered the same problem you have, or soon will: No one would talk to me. Especially now, with the new HIPPA regulations in place, mental health professionals are more and more often saying things like, "I can't even confirm that your brother is a patient of mine, much less talk to you!" It's enough to make you want to scream. And yet, this obstacle is not coming from an evil place, nor is it unmovable.

If you are a family member, remind the therapist that you can share your observations and concern without violating confidentiality laws

If you are a family member, you can share your observations without violating the doctor-patient relationship. If someone tells you he or she can't talk with you, say "I know you can't, and that's not what I am asking you to do. I am not even asking you to verify that my loved one is your patient. All I am asking is that you let me share some observations and concerns about my loved one. All I ask is that you listen for a minute." There are no regulations prohibiting a therapist from listening! Try it and you will see that it opens at least half the line of communication. The other half, getting the therapist to talk with you, requires that you do something further.

As I mentioned earlier, therapists can pave the way for this type of collaboration by clarifying the limits of confidentiality with their patient up front. (i.e.," I would like to hear from your family from time to time to get a feel for how they think you're doing. Also, if you become sick, I may want to talk with them to get their help."). The bottom line is that if the patient knows that certain types of communication will occur between doctor and family, confidentiality is not being violated. The rules have to be a little different when you are dealing with serious mental illnesses because judgment and insight can become severely impaired. That's why we all need to talk to one another and work as a team.

When families work actively with the treatment team, they increase the quality of care. It's not something we're proud of, but most doctors and therapists will feel more accountable when a family member is actively involved. Better yet, we become much better at detecting and responding to any worsening of the illness than when we work in isolation.

When I give talks I often discuss the vital importance of building a "Treatment Triad." What I mean by this is building teamwork among the consumer, his loved one, and the mental health professional. When all three are working together, stabilization and/or recovery become much more likely. To become more effective at building a treatment team, you must overcome some common barriers, including the ones I mentioned above. Also, you must identify personal barriers such as your own negative preconceptions about "the other side."

If you're a therapist, you have to overcome your preconceived belief that family members may distract you from your work. One misconception I have had is that family members call me to vent and get free therapy. I am not proud of that thought, but I often have it when I am ending a very long day and a family member wants to talk to me about how hard their relative's illness has been on them. Of course I understand and sympathize, but that's not the point. The problem is that, if you have more than one patient (which we all do), it's impossible to be available to all your patients' involved family members in this way. What I have learned, however, is that if I explain my limitations and suggest that the stressed relative think about getting help for him- or herself, it helps to refocus the conversation on what we should be talking about. If the family member is unwilling to get professional help, I will strongly suggest he or she go to a NAMI meeting to gain support from other people in the same situation.

If you're a family member, you may make the mistake of thinking that an unresponsive therapist (one who won't return phone calls, won't talk to you, etc.) doesn't care. I can't tell you that you would be wrong, but I can say that in my experience this assumption is more likely than not incorrect. Most therapists (RNs, MSWs, Ph.D.s, Psy.D.s and, yes, even M.D.s) got into this line of work because they care. They chose the career because, like me, it has personal meaning for them and they want to help. But if that's the case, why do they sometimes appear so uncaring? In short, the reason is often "burn out." That said, however, you can help by being focused on specific issues when you call (e.g., "I want to tell you about some warning signs of relapse I am seeing." Or "I am concerned about the discharge plan because..."). Don't call to vent. Call a friend, relative, or your own therapist to get that kind of support.

Finding and using a mobile crisis team

While maintaining contact and working with doctors is the best possible solution, doing that not always possible. If you are dealing with a loved one who is an adult, who has never been committed, and who refuses to see a doctor, you may find that you have no one to call. Even if this is the situation, however, you needn't feel that you are alone or have only the police as a resource. That was, in fact, my situation when Henry was committed for the first time. What I didn't take advantage of, however, is the fact that most hospitals with a psychiatric care unit also have a mobile crisis team. This team is usually made up of Master's level psychologists, social workers, or nurses who perform home visits. Like paramedics, they're typically in close contact with a doctor who is stationed in the psychiatric emergency room. Mobile crisis teams are trained to evaluate, refer to outpatient treatment, and, if necessary, hospitalize. To find out whether your community has a mobile crisis team, you should call your local hospital and ask for the psychiatric emergency room. Usually, a psychiatric nurse will answer your call, or, if not, the psychiatrist on call. Explain that you are concerned about a loved one and ask what resources are available. The nurse or doctor will be able to tell you about the mobile crisis team and how to contact them. Add this number to your list of doctors and emergency numbers. Sometimes just knowing that it is there can be a relief.

You will also be able to ask about other outpatient services in your community. Even if you haven't reached a crisis point with your loved one, you should feel free to call the psychiatric emergency room or any other local mental health facility. Don't worry about interrupting someone in the middle of an emergency. If you have, he or she will let you know and ask you to call back. When I was covering the psychiatric emergency room during my training, I spent as much time fielding such calls as I did evaluating patients in the ER.

Calling 911 and asking for CIT officers

If you call 911, be sure to ask if the law enforcement department you have reached (metro police, sheriff's department, highway patrol, etc.) if they have a Crisis Intervention Team (CIT). Many now do and many more will have them by the time this book hits the presses. Ask specifically for a CIT trained unit to respond.

CIT officers have been trained in how to separate criminal behavior from mental illness and more importantly, how to communicate effectively with an agitated person suffering from psychosis. At LEAP Institute we have provided adjunctive training seminars for CIT officers around the country. In my experience those officers who volunteer for the extra training – as much as 40 hours of additional classroom time involving reading, lectures and role-plays — are compassionate, understanding and have the skills to help calm someone who is psychotic and paranoid or simply frightened. They arrive at the scene with safety first and foremost on their mind but also with an understanding that they are dealing with a person who has mental illness and who needs first and foremost to be listened to, calmed down and convinced to come safely and quietly for an evaluation.

The evaluation

After you take your loved one to the hospital or call the mobile crisis team or CIT officers, you should immediately ask to speak with the doctor who conducted or supervised the evaluation. There are several reasons why it is important for you to speak with the doctor in charge of your loved one's case sooner rather than later. The first is the obvious reason discussed above: You are forming a team with the doctors to insure that your loved one gets the care that he needs. There is currently no cure for serious mental illnesses, so it's a good idea to build a network of people who will be familiar with you and your loved one.

Another reason to make sure you talk with the doctor in charge may sound a bit cynical, but it is not. It is realistic. Sometimes doctors working in hospitals don't have the time or resources to give everyone the quality of attention that may be warranted. If you are a mental health professional, it is usually easier to get the doctor's attention. If you are a family member, you may be asked to call back in the morning. In either case, don't be put off. Act as you would if you were dealing with an accident or the flare-up of some other medical illness like heart disease. In these instances you would no doubt approach the doctor to find out all the details of the diagnosis, prognosis, and treatment. Find out what's going on and what the plan is. If nothing else is gained, you will at least have let the doctor know that his patient is your loved one and that you hold him accountable for the care that is given.

The doctor who does the diagnosis and intake for your loved one is going to be your biggest ally if your loved one needs to stay in the hospital longer stay than the 72 hours generally mandated by an emergency commitment. The three-day holding period is all that many states allow without some kind of civil court hearing. The admitting doctor is experienced with the commitment procedure for your state. The length of stay ordered will depend, in large part, on the recommendations of the doctors caring for your loved one.

One final word about calling the police

The idea of having to call the police for help with a loved one seems very dramatic and somehow wrong. We usually call the police when a crime has been committed. However, you may need to call the police when your loved one is out of control because they're the ones trained to act in situations where someone is not in control of his behavior.

Not all police departments offer CIT training. If your local police department does not offer such training, contact the Memphis Tennessee police department to learn of their crisis intervention program or check with the websites I gave you above. The Memphis Police Department's CIT program was recognized at a White House conference in 1999 as a model system for "decriminalizing" the mentally ill. Ask for literature and pass it along to your local police. I was fortunate in that when I called the Tucson police about my brother in the early 1980s they had received such specialized training. Nevertheless, whenever I called the police to ask for help getting my brother to the hospital, my mother would become angry with me. She felt protective of Henry and believed that involving the police was somehow criminalizing him.

If you had a five-year-old child who ran into the street, you would pick him up and restrain him. If he had a temper tantrum and threatened to harm you, you would send him to his room.

One explanation I gave my mother then and have since given many family members and mental health professionals is the following: If you had a five-year-old child who ran into the street, you would pick him up and restrain him. If he had a temper tantrum and threatened to harm you, you would probably send him to his room. When someone is a full-grown adult, you can't physically do any of these things. But the police can.

In my experience, police officers usually restrain and transport people with mental illness with respect and dignity.

In my experience, police officers usually restrain and transport mentally ill people with respect and dignity. If you feel that your local police force has not received the training they need to elevate their understanding and sensitivity to persons with serious mental illness, contact your police chief, sheriff, or police commissioner and suggest that they learn about the model used by the Memphis police department (see www.NAMI.org for information).

Very often, when you call the police, there will be a scene. Your loved one will resist being taken to the hospital, but that isn't always the case. Sometimes the police come and are not able to help because everything looks fairly normal and calm. I used to work on a mobile crisis team, and we would call this sudden calmness the "ambulance cure." We coined the phrase after evaluating a man with schizophrenia who had been screaming threats at the top of his lungs in a 24-hour convenience store. He accused the clerks of spying on him and demanded that they stop.

He was delusional and hearing voices that he told us about when we arrived. After conferring with the psychiatrist at the hospital on our radios, we all agreed that he should be brought in for a 72-hour observation period. However, by the time the ambulance arrived to transport him to the hospital, he was visibly calmer. And by the time he was being evaluated by the ER psychiatrist, he was denying that any of it had happened. He knew that if he talked about the voices or his paranoid fears the doctor would admit him to the hospital. And since he didn't think he was ill and didn't want to stay, he avoided the topics he knew would get him admitted. Fortunately, the psychiatrists we worked with trusted our judgment and did not make rash decisions. After three hours in the ER, he began to get agitated again. He started mumbling to his voices and talking about his concern that the clerks had bugged the interview room.

If your loved one has calmed down by the time the police arrive, be sure to tell them everything that happened in detail. If threats were made, don't be shy about talking about them. If furniture was turned over and dishes broken, don't straighten up prior to their arrival. Be certain to tell them that they're dealing with someone who has a history of serious mental illness and that you are very concerned for his safety. Ask them to take your loved one to the hospital if they don't offer to do so. If they refuse, ask to speak with their supervisor.

Below are some tips to help you when you call the police:

- *Always ask first for a CIT officer (remember the department you reach may not have such a program yet)*
- *Remember that police officers are often, but not always, trained to deal with someone who is mentally ill.*
- *Make it clear to the dispatcher that the situation involves someone who is mentally ill. That way the police will be aware of what they're walking into.*

- *If possible, meet the police at the door, tell them where your loved one is, why you are concerned, and what kind of behavior they will encounter when they enter.*
- *Be sure to tell them whether or not your loved one has access to any type of weapon. If there is no weapon, the officers will be less anxious and can focus first on the safety of your loved one. If there is a weapon, they need to know.*
- *If your loved one has thrown or broken anything, don't try to clean up before the police come. Whatever damage your loved has caused may be the only overt sign of illness the officers can see.*

Finally, if you need to call the police to help you with your loved one, please don't blame yourself for doing something awful or inappropriate. The police regularly respond to situations involving people who are seriously mentally ill. Also, remember that you are not alone. The Resources section at the back of this book lists organizations that help families who are dealing with mental illness, and many of the web sites offer personal accounts of how other people have handled the same or similar situations.

14

How to Survive an Involuntary Treatment

Even if you believe that seeking an involuntary commitment was the best thing for your loved one, you will probably suffer some emotional fallout. You know that your loved one is sick and you know that, at least for the time being, forcing him to take medication was imperative and maybe the only chance he will ever have to get better. But he is likely to feel betrayed by what you have done and to be not very open to talking with you about why you did what you did. Worse yet, you may feel that he is right. If either of you believes you have acted like a Judas, there can be no partnership or treatment agreement. That is one of the reasons that dealing with his feelings of betrayal is vital. The other reason, of course, is to regain trust and preserve your relationship.

During the initial days your loved one is in the hospital, it is only natural that he will be angry with you. Wouldn't you be angry if you thought you were not ill and someone had called the police on you, resulting in your being forced into a psychiatric ward? I would be furious! Add to the anger the fact that your loved one is probably sicker than usual (otherwise, why do what you did?) and it may not be possible for you to have a meaningful conversation just yet.

It is imperative that you visit as often as you can without overburdening yourself.

This doesn't mean that you should avoid going to the hospital to visit. Sometimes well meaning hospital staff may encourage you to wait if they feel you will be upset to see your loved one so ill. Other times, your loved one may refuse to see you. But it is, nevertheless, imperative that you visit as often as you can without overburdening yourself. The reason for this is that many people who are forced into the hospital feel that their families want to get rid of them and have abandoned them. It's harder for them to believe this if you try to visit the hospital every day, or close to that, even if it's only for five minutes to say, "Hi, I love you."

During Henry's first real hospitalization, after the time he had been turned away at the E.R., he refused to speak with me when I visited. I remember the first time I walked in. He was sitting in front of the television in the common room (called the "day room" in most hospitals). When I went over to him and said hi, he gave me one quick angry look, got up, and went directly to his room. I asked the nurse to get him, but she reported that he didn't want to talk with me and suggested I leave. Nevertheless, over the next two weeks I went back again and again despite the fact that I mostly sat in the day room and read the newspaper. It was a long drive to the hospital, so I figured I might as well make the most of my effort and stay a while. More than that, however, I also felt very guilty about what had happened and hoped that if I stayed long enough Henry might come out of his room and agree to talk with me. Eventually, he did, and at the time I had the good sense to apologize. Although, as I've said, I did some stupid things as well, that apology was a vital first-step toward repairing the damage done by the involuntary hospitalization.

When I encourage you to visit, however, I'm basing my recommendation not only on my experience as a family member but also on my experience as a doctor who has worked in several wards like the one my brother was in. I see how patients react when family does not visit. I see how easy it is to feed the seeds of feeling betrayed and how that affects what happens after discharge from the hospital. So, do your best to visit regularly, but, at the same time, you need to remember to take care of yourself during this period. If trips to the hospital are draining and too overwhelming, stay just for the few minutes it takes for your loved one to see that you are there and haven't abandoned him. Then go home and try to relax, watch a movie, go out to dinner with a close friend. Letting yourself brood endlessly about what's going on in the hospital will not help anyone and can be detrimental to you and your relationship with your loved one. If you are not seeing a therapist of your own, this may be a good opportunity for you to find someone you can talk to about your situation. Family organizations like NAMI are particularly helpful in this regard.

At some point during or after the hospitalization, you will need to begin looking for an opportunity to talk with your loved one about what happened. It is very important that you talk about what you did and also about how it made your loved one feel. There is no perfect script for what you should say in this conversation other than making certain that you are speaking from your heart and touching on the themes I describe below. It may be as simple as when I said to my brother, "I had to call the police. I couldn't have lived with myself if I didn't." Or, "I know you feel angry and betrayed, but I would have felt guilty and as if I had let you down if I didn't get you into the hospital."

Turning betrayal into loyalty

A conversation aimed at dealing with feelings of betrayal should always start with an apology and the statement that you understand how your loved one feels. "I know you don't feel you needed this, I know you are angry with me, I'm very sorry that what I've done is so hurtful to you, but I would like to tell you why I felt I had to do it." In large part, this conversation is more of an apology than a justification, and you need to be careful not to become accusatory or defensive in any way. Acknowledge your loved one's feelings of betrayal while pointing out that you were following your conscience.

I am not recommending that you apologize for what you did, but rather for how it made your loved one feel.

You may balk at the notion of apologizing. After all, you were acting in your loved one's best interest so you have nothing to be sorry for. I agree. I am not recommending that you apologize for what you did, but rather for how it made your loved one feel. You and I would feel the same way and appreciate the empathy that is conveyed with an apology.

Here are some general Dos and Don'ts to help you to have a conversation that will aid in mending the relationship.

Do
1. Acknowledge his feelings of betrayal.
2. Ask for forgiveness.
3. Explain why you felt you had to do what you did.
4. Be honest that you would do it again.

Don't
1. Deny his feelings of betrayal.
2. Expect to be forgiven right away.
3. Blame your loved one for what you felt you had to do.
4. Be misleading about what you would do in the future.

There are four main points you should try to convey to your loved one: your regret, your fear that he will be angry with you and not understand your perspective, why you felt you had to take the actions that you did, and an appeal for his forgiveness.

1. Regret

It is very natural that you may feel regret about "locking-up" your loved one. It's not unlike the regret we feel whenever we impose a restriction on a child (e.g., when you tell a child "go to your room"). The fact that it was done with the best of intentions doesn't mean that it was easy to do or that you are not sorry you felt you had to do it.

When you have the conversation with your loved one, let him know that you regret having had to commit him and wish you hadn't had to do it. But don't blame your loved one for putting you in the position of having to do something you'd rather not have done; this will only lead to estrangement, not an alliance. Instead, simply state your feelings. You feel sorry that your conscience led you to do something you know your loved one felt was hurtful. In the space below, write down any feelings of regret you have about the commitment and how you might say this to your loved one.

Did you write something you will be able to convey to your loved one in a way that helps him understand the dilemma you were in? Put yourself in the shoes of your loved one for a moment and read what you wrote. Is it something you would respond to well? Would you feel blamed? Or do you feel that you would understand how the person who committed you felt about doing it?

〳〳

Emphasize that your values and love led you to do what you did, not that you were "right" to do it.

〳〳

Don't speak in absolute truths like, "I had to do this; I had no other choice." Instead say, "I *felt* I had to do this, I *felt* I had no other choice." Emphasize that your values and love led you to do what you did, not that you were "right" to do it. After I learned to talk to my brother in this way (today he very rarely is hospitalized and almost never against his will) I would say, "I wish I didn't feel the way I do, I am so sorry that I pushed this on you. I know you don't agree with my view but I hope you can forgive me. I only did this because I felt it was the right thing and because I love you." From there, the conversation generally went something like this.

"If you loved me you would never have called the police on me! I am angry!"

"Henry, I would feel the same way."

"Then why did you do it?"

"Because—and I wish I didn't feel this way because I know it's hurtful to you—but because I was scared and felt you needed to be in the hospital."

"You've been brainwashed by the psychiatrists. There's nothing wrong with me."

"I understand and respect your perspective. Do you get mine?"

"You were scared and thought you were trying to help me," Henry said.

"Right. And I am really sorry we're so far apart on this but glad you can at least understand that however misguided you think I am, my intentions were good. Do you believe that?"

"I do," he said, much to my relief.

By empathizing and normalizing (saying "I would feel the same way") his experience of what I had done to him, I opened the door to Henry's being able to see the important truth, which is that, regardless of who was right (him or me) about his being sick, I did what I did because *I felt* it was the right thing to do and because I loved him.

2. Fear

Explain what it is you were afraid would happen if you didn't have your loved one committed. Preface your fears by acknowledging that your loved one did not share your concern (e.g., "I know you weren't worried about..."). Then ask if he would like to hear what you were worried about (e.g., "Can I tell you why I was worried?").

As you explain the fears you had, it is important that you phrase them in such a way that you are not making accusations about anticipated behavior. Also, explain that your fears grew out of the fact that you care for him so deeply, not from expecting him to behave badly. Keeping in mind what was said above, write down a few of the fears you think you could share with your loved to help him understand your motivations and mend the relationship.

||||||||||||||||||||||||||||||||||||||||||||||||||||||||||||||||||||||||||||||||||||||||||||||||||||||||||||||||||||||||||||||||||||||||||||||||

||||||||||||||||||||||||||||||||||||||||||||||||||||||||||||||||||||||||||||||||||||||||||||||||||||||||||||||||||||||||||||||||||||||||||||||||

Have a look at what you wrote and refer to the dos and don'ts given above. Did you follow the advice I gave? How would you feel if the tables were turned and you were hearing your words played back to you? If you think you would feel cared for and not defensive, you are on the right track.

_____

Don't ask him to agree; ask only that he understand and
forgive you for following your conscience.

_____

3. Actions

Explain why you took the actions you did. Remind your loved one of the event(s) that precipitated your calling the police (or crisis team) or taking him to the hospital. In my case with Henry, it was his expressing suicidal thoughts and my fear that he would harm himself. As you write down the reasons for your actions keep in mind that you don't want to sound accusing or angry. This is a conversation in which you are trying to convey your reasons for having your loved one committed. Don't ask him to agree; ask only that he understand and forgive you for following your conscience. In the space provided, write down the reasons you pursued a commitment.

_____

_____

By now you know what I am going to ask. Have a look at what you wrote and see if you followed the dos and don'ts given above. Next, ask yourself how you would feel if the tables were turned and you were hearing your words played back to you. Would you feel like arguing against the points made or would you be able to hear them without getting defensive?

4. Appeal for forgiveness and understanding

What you are asking your loved one to do is try to comprehend why you did what you had to do, how much you love him, and how much his forgiveness means to you. Don't be afraid to let him have the upper hand. In other words, stand firmly on your convictions but don't try to justify yourself or your decision. After all, you won! Think of the power you wielded. Your loved one was forced to take medicine **(how can he be forced to take medicine *without* being forced into the hospital?)** or forced into a hospital against his will. You can afford to be magnanimous. You are asking your loved one to forgive you; that is all. Listen carefully to what he has to say and see where the dialogue leads.

If your loved one refuses to talk with you about the commitment, write it all down in a letter

Don't expect to be successful after only one conversation. It will take several discussions before your loved one's misconceptions about how you feel and why you did what you did can be corrected. If your loved one refuses to talk with you about the commitment, write it all down in a letter. In fact, even if you have had successful discussions, it's useful to write a letter that covers the four points discussed above. Serious mental illness sometimes makes it difficult for people to remember. Having your explanation and appeal for forgiveness in writing will help your loved one remember what you said.

I wish I could end this chapter by saying that if you follow all the above steps you will have turned your loved one's feelings of betrayal into feelings of understanding and empathy for your predicament. But that would be unrealistic. Whether your loved one is able to forgive, let go of feeling betrayed, and understand your point of view will rely in large part on his innate capacity to accomplish these things. However, I can promise that if you follow the advice given here, you will feel better about what you have done and reduce the degree of conflict in your relationship with your loved one.

15
The Surprise

I'm sure you remember that one of the first things I told you, way back at the beginning of this book, was that your goal was *not* to get your loved one to admit he or she was sick but to get him to follow his statement "I'm not sick," with the statement "But, I could use some help." In other words, the techniques I've been teaching you are not aimed at getting the person who is mentally ill to gain insight into being ill; they are directed specifically at getting him to find reasons to accept treatment despite what he believes.

If you've reached the point where your patient or loved one has made that commitment, what you want to do now is make sure *you* don't revert to old bad habits like giving your opinion without first asking if the other person wants to hear it. You need to maintain and build on the collaborative dialogue you've begun, and while you may be tempted to remind the mentally ill person that "doctor knows best," or, even worse, "father knows best," you've got to remember that those so-called wise words aren't going to make one bit of difference to the one you're trying to help. In fact, they will more than likely just blow up the bridge you've so carefully been building between you.

But you know all that already, right? So what's the surprise? The surprise is that when people with a serious mental illness are in treatment, and when they have the kind of relationship I've been trying to help you build with them—one that allows them to feel their point of view is respected and to trust you—they *will* begin to develop insight.

Remember Vicky, whose interview with Dr. Kohut you read in Chapter 6? Initially, Vicky continued to believe she was "cured" of bipolar disorder but agreed to continue taking her lithium on a trial basis for 6 months and then, if she decided to go off it, to do so in conjunction with her doctor. She was able to make this commitment because Dr. Kohut had allowed her to understand that she was, ultimately, the one in charge of whether or not she would take the medicine. By doing that he had won her trust and shown her that he honored and respected her feelings. After a while Vicky was also able to see what happened when she lowered her dose or discontinued her medication, and she gained true insight into the relationship between taking the medication and remaining asymptomatic. When she recognized that without the lithium she was getting "worn out" again, she *asked* to be put back on medication.

And then there was Dolores, who kept losing jobs because she was holding conversations aloud with the voices in her head. At first Dolores didn't see any relationship between her getting fired and going off her medication. In fact, she initially believed that the medication was *making* her hear voices. It took a long time, and several more hospitalizations, but Dolores did gradually come to have some insight into the fact that when she stopped taking medication she talked to herself more, and that this was likely to make people think she was "nuts." Like Vicky, she developed insight into how medications helped her with a problem she was having. Vicky didn't call the problem bipolar disorder; she called it getting "worn out." Dolores's problem, as she saw it, wasn't having hallucinations; it was talking aloud to herself. Nevertheless, both these women developed insight into how the medications helped them with their problems as *they* saw them. The surprise, then, is that over time people do begin to redefine their problems as mental illness, whether or not they define mental illness in exactly the same way you do.

In psychology, we call this the change paradox. When you stop pushing someone to change, often they find reasons to change all on their own. I think that is what happened not only with Vicky and Dolores but also with other patients who have benefited from the kind of relationship I've been talking about while taking their medications. Given the room to explore their situation with someone they trusted and who did not preach or tell them they were sick, they were able to develop insight. First the insight was about positive outcomes linked to taking medicine and then later, into having a mental illness.

We know today, right now, that building a respectful and trusting relationship is the key to helping someone with poor insight accept treatment for mental illness.

I think the anecdotal evidence is pretty compelling, but there are also scientific studies to show that developing the kinds of relationships I've been talking about can and does ameliorate lack of insight in patients with serious mental illness. In a study by Dr. Roisen Kemp and her colleagues, published in the *British Journal of Psychiatry* in 1998, the researchers found that medication adherence and insight improved over an 18 month follow-up period after only six sessions of MET. Remember, LEAP is based on MET which seeks to create a collaborative relationship with the person in "denial". This is one good example of how building the mutually respectful and trusting relationships we have been talking about can help with both adherence and insight. And, as I mentioned in Chapter 10, new research on medication may also help in our battle against anosognosia. Regardless of what happens with the research on medication, however, we know today, right now, that building a respectful and trusting relationship is the key to helping someone with poor insight accept treatment for mental illness.

Whether you are a family member or a mental health provider, what this means is that when you create a nonjudgmental and trusting relationship, the person you are trying to help will find reasons to be in treatment, and over time, develop insight about having a mental illness. It may take a year or two of staying in treatment, but the pay-off over a lifetime is incalculable.

As you go forward, however, you need to remember that you are a member of the team. You need to be strong and well rested. If you do more than you should, you will lose motivation and risk "burn-out." Burn-out is a term used by mental health professionals to describe the feeling of complete exhaustion that comes from having been immersed in other peoples' problems for too long. Exhausting yourself will only make you less effective and your loved one or patient feel like a burden.

If you are a family member, I want to add one final word from one family member to another. You are in a unique position to help your loved one learn how to cope with mental illness. You knew your loved one before the illness struck, which means that you know the core person who is often eclipsed by symptoms of the disease. And when someone who is seriously mentally ill feels that you see him for who he is, not just for the diagnosis he has been given, he will be open to learning from you.

The Surprise for Henry and Xavier

Henry never developed insight into being mentally ill. But the last time I saw him, in the days following our mother's funeral, I can't tell you how much comfort I received from him because it was more visceral than verbal; I know he felt the same. Yes we talked, but our shared battles, betrayals and ultimately our reconciliation, made possible by our respect for each other, was something we felt in our bones. That was three years ago. On the drive back to his house, on our last night together, my brother told me he felt I saw him for who he was. Henry was very kind, smart, funny, insightful (about most things), and creative. Yes he was a pain in the ass (and I to him) during the early years of his illness when we argued about whether or not he was mentally ill and needed treatment. But I was to blame for that more than he. Henry was able to laugh at life. I saw him and liked him and he knew that.

I learned a lot from my brother---a man most people gave a wide berth to because of his explosive eruptions into laughter for no apparent reason and his conversations with the voices only he heard. He taught me how to throw a baseball, ride a bicycle, and the power of humility. When we were growing up, he brought humor and magic into my life (like the time, when I was five, that he convinced me I had just missed Santa Claus flying by our window). More recently, he taught me about compassion, patience, perseverance and most importantly, forgiveness. I feel very fortunate, as you will read in the next section, that we had a strong friendship for many years before he died.

LEAP would not exist if not for Henry Amador. It was not my creation alone or that of my collaboration with Aaron (Tim) Beck, M.D. and other colleagues and patients. More than anyone else Henry helped me to develop LEAP and without it, I am sure we would have lost many years of closeness, laughter and love.

In the next, and last, section of this book I give you the details of where LEAP comes from theoretically, a summary of recent research on cognitive behavioral therapy for schizophrenia (which LEAP draws on in part) and a review of recent research on the link between violence and poor adherence. I next make an argument for why we must include anosognosia in our diagnostic manual, not only for schizophrenia, but for other psychotic disorders. And finally, I tell you the end of Henry's story. Perhaps "end" is not the correct word because I believe that with every copy of this book that is read his story continues to unfold and his example: his compassion, empathy and kindness, continues to help others reach people with serious mental illness and bring them back to their families and communities.

Part IV

Theory, Research and Practical Advice on LEAP

16
LEAP Theory and Research

The first edition of this book described LEAP in 2000. However, LEAP draws from preexisting psychotherapeutic traditions that date back 50 years.LEAP has three major influences: Carl Rogers Client-Centered Therapy, Aaron T. Beck's Cognitive Therapy and Miller and Rollnick's Motivational Interviewing.

Carl Rogers Client-Centered Therapy (1951, 1959)

LEAP is partly based on Rogers's conception of the transformative power of "actively listening" to patients:

"Real communication occurs...when we listen with understanding. What does this mean? It means to see the expressed idea and attitude from the other person's point of view, to sense how it feels to him, to achieve his frame of reference in regard to the thing he is talking about." (Carl Rogers, 1961; *On Becoming a Person*, Mariner Books, page 332)

The main idea is that judgment or evaluation is a barrier to constructive communication. The better you listen the less you judge. When the patient feels understood, he feels trust and openness to the therapist.

Among the main lessons I learned from Client-Centered Therapy was that I should give up the directive-expert perspective, communicate respect for the client's views, listen actively and show empathy.

Aaron Beck's cognitive therapy (1979)

In 1979, Aaron T. Beck, in his book *Cognitive Therapy of Depression* highlights that specific dysfunctional cognitive patterns lead to, or sustain, mental disorders. However, to listen is not enough in order to modify these specific dysfunctional cognitive patterns (called schema). Cognitive therapy offers many techniques that are helpful to improve a patient's engagement into the interaction and ultimately treatment. Thus, when working on the issue of adherence to treatment the therapist should:

- Take a collaborative stance
- Use mutually agreed on agendas
- Explore disadvantages and advantages of medication and services
- Define goals that the patient is willing to work on

Among the many lessons I learned from Cognitive Therapy that were incorporated into LEAP was the importance of creating structure when possible such as beginning meetings with setting an agenda — but staying flexible. Attempt to create an agenda for conversations either by following the patient's lead (e.g., "You were just talking about how angry you are that the police picked you up, can we talk about that today?) or introducing ideas (e.g., "You mentioned not liking medication, can we talk about that?). Remember to ask questions. This LEAP rule came from cognitive therapy. Cognitive therapy is very collaborative as is LEAP and the therapist frequently "checks in" with the patient to find out what is perceived as helpful and what is not. Importantly, cognitive therapy also relies on conducting cost/benefit analysis with the client---just as we do in LEAP---whenever possible.

Motivational Interviewing (1991)

"Motivational Interviewing, or Motivational Enhancement Therapy (MET) is an approach to helping people change that was originally developed by William R. Miller and Stephen Rollnick. It directly addresses a significant problem common to all therapies: resistance to change. In MET, resistance is seen as a result of ambivalence about change. Its primary goals are to help clients increase their intrinsic motivation and resolve ambivalence in order to facilitate behavior change." Hal Arkowitz et al., (2008) *Motivational Interviewing in the treatment of psychological problems*, London: The Guilford Press, Page ix.

In Motivational Interviewing, the therapist is a guide that asks questions, listens and ultimately informs his patients. As you will see, LEAP was influenced mainly by these first two components of Motivational Interviewing. Importantly, LEAP differs from MET in its approach to informing (i.e., giving an opinion, making recommendations or educating). Like in MI, LEAP's main focus is to obtain collaboration from the patient by showing respect for his autonomy and opinions even when they are at odds with the therapist's.

The main idea is that the therapist should adopt a guiding style (e.g., use open ended questions) rather than a controlling or directive one in order to promote a more active involvement in the interaction. Consequently, the therapist strives to:

- Guide (open questions) rather than press,
- Assess motivation for change,
- Support client's self-efficacy,
- Assess previous attempts to fix the problem,
- Talk in hypothetical language for patients who are less ready to change,
- Collaboratively explore ambivalence to motivate the process of behavior change.

Among the lessons learned from MET is to not direct. LEAP takes this a big step further in that we encourage you to show genuine reluctance to direct—to give your opinion. Like MET, LEAP also capitalizes on those aspects of insight the person has and ignores those that appear deeply ingrained (such as the belief "I am not sick"). Instead, we focus on the desire to change certain things in the person's life, to articulate and strive for goals and to resolve ambivalence about getting help to achieve those goals.

Summary

In Carl Rogers' Client-Centered Therapy as well as in Motivational Interviewing, the process of building an alliance starts by focusing on understanding the patient's perspectives and problems. Understanding the patient's perspective is central to the LEAP approach.Understanding and communicating it accurately is considered the key to transforming an adversarial relationship into an alliance. As opposed to Roger's Client Centered Therapy as well as Beck's Cognitive Therapy, however, MET focuses on listening to/and working on ambivalence and change talk. Change talk is based on the patient's desires, ability, reasons and need for change.

What the patient **desires** ("what do you want?")

The patient's **ability** ("What can you do?")

The **reasons** for change ("Why would you do it? Why would you change?")

The **need** for change ("How much do you need to change?")

In short LEAP utilizes the following tools and principles from the three therapies:

From Roger's client-centered therapy: reflective listening as the foundation for creating an alliance. Central to this technique is a complete lack of judgment – no opinion about what is being said is given unless it has been asked for (preferably many times over).

From Cognitive Therapy: The collaborative stance, setting an agenda and cost benefit analyses.

From MI: The patient remains the final arbiter of the change process. Ambivalence about change is explored. And perhaps most importantly, internal and external motivators (or desires) are identified.

I admit it, LEAP is not entirely new; its main principals are familiar and so sometimes people say "LEAP is just like..." not so much accusing me of plagiarism as much as recognizing the heritage. The American folk singer Woody Guthrie, writer of the song "This Land is Your Land," which we all learned as children, was sometimes accused of stealing the melodies for his songs from old gospel tunes. In fact, he had never tried to hide his practice of borrowing from melodies that had already been written, saying, "There are no new melodies; they ' re all used up!" I feel that way about most useful insights into human psychology and relations. LEAP is new but, like Guthrie's songs, it relies on what came before – from certain philosophical traditions, from the three therapies I summarized above, and from common sense. It is a method for easily remembering and using age-old truths in your everyday life. Like a melody that is catchy and hard to forget, once you learn LEAP you will find that you can call it up any time you need it.

Recent Research on LEAP

Next, I briefly describe the results of a study my colleagues Celine Paillot, Ph.D., Raymond Goetz Ph.D., and I published in the National Institute of Mental Health's Journal *Schizophrenia Bulletin*. The study was presented at the International Congress on Schizophrenia Research in June of 2009. Although Dr. Goetz and I consulted with her and published the study together, Dr. Paillot conducted the study herself while pursuing her doctorate degree at the University of Paris X.

As stated earlier, most patients with DSM-IV diagnosed schizophrenia exhibit full or partial non-adherence to pharmacological treatment (Rummel-Kluge, 2008). Only about one-third reliably take antipsychotic medication as prescribed (Oehl, 2000). Poor adherence (i.e., both complete and partial non adherence) has been found to be associated with relapse, increased involuntary admissions, poorer course of illness, and increased incidence of violence and suicide (Amador and David 2004). Given the serious outcomes associated with poor adherence interventions aimed at improving and maintaining adherence are of great interest to clinicians, researchers, and policy makers.

The main aim of our study was to assess the efficacy of LEAP when compared to a control intervention. The study involved 54 patients diagnosed with schizophrenia about to be discharged following inpatient treatment. Patients were randomly assigned to either the experimental or control therapies. Subjects did not know whether they were receiving the experimental versus control therapy which was essentially Carl Roger's Client Centered Therapy as described above. All patients were treated with long acting injectable antipsychotic medications (either typical or atypical) and rated as compliant when the injection was confirmed and non compliant if the injection was refused or the appointment for the injection was missed. Insight into schizophrenia and attitudes toward treatment were assessed using the Scale to assess Unawareness of Mental Disorder, the Birchwood Insight Scale and the Drug Attitude Inventory, respectively. All assessments were made by a single rater who was blind to group assignment.

The results show that compared to Roger's therapy LEAP improved motivation for change, insight and adherence to treatment. This study found LEAP to be superior to the control psychotherapy. It improved compliance, motivation for change, insight and attitudes towards treatment. Among the strengths of the experimental design was the fact that we used randomized blinded group assignment, blinded assessments of the dependent variables and near 100% reliability and validity of the adherence measure. Among the limitations of the study was the absence of a LEAP fidelity measure and the fact that the senior author (Dr. Paillot) was the only therapist for all patients and as such could have inadvertently biased the results by differentially treating patients depending on which therapy they were assigned to. We are currently planning to attempt a replication of this study in a larger more heterogeneous sample with a longitudinal assessment of fidelity to the LEAP intervention and therapists blinded to study hypotheses.

17

Psychotherapy for Psychosis?

As I have written in Chapter 1, and previously in a column I write for *Schizophrenia Magazine*,[14] about 50% of persons with schizophrenia have great difficulty seeing that they have a mental illness (i.e., they have the symptom of anosognosia) and this lack of awareness is linked to frontal lobe dysfunction. As such it does not change—insight does not increase---easily over time.

The data supporting this statement are so well replicated that ten years ago the diagnostic manual all North American doctors and mental health professionals use reported these facts (see page 304 of the *DSM-IV-TR*, American Psychiatric Association Press, 2000). In addition, as I wrote earlier, many persons with schizophrenia and bipolar disorder either refuse, or take only a small portion of, the medication prescribed (estimates are from 50 to 75%). And for those persons who understand that they have an illness and take medication, not all respond to the treatment or respond only partially (e.g., the voices are diminished but the delusions persist). So if many people refuse medication, or

14. Portions of this chapter and some of the chapters to follow appeared, in part, in the column I write for *Schizophrenia Magazine*, published by Magpie Publishing (*www. szmagazine.com*). The publisher has kindly given me permission to reproduce excerpts from this work here. Schizophrenia Magazine is an informative, inspiring and novel resource for consumers, their families and clinicians. I highly recommend it to you and not just because I write a column for them! In fact, the only reason I write the column is because of my high opinion of this magazine. I also volunteer my time to serve on their Editorial Board and wouldn't do so if I did not think my time spent was well worth the effort.

take only sub-therapeutic doses, and medication does not always work for those who do take it as prescribed, what can be done?

So if many people refuse medication, or take only sub-therapeutic doses... what can be done?

Although I pose it as a question in the title of this chapter, I have no doubt that as a field we need to offer psychotherapy to most, if not all, persons with psychosis. In this chapter I will highlight some of the research on Cognitive Behavioral Therapy (CBT) in psychosis. I will also briefly discuss Motivational Interviewing which I consider a "close cousin" of CBT and argue that strong support exists for their effectiveness in increasing adherence to medication, improving some aspects of insight into illness, lowering the severity of some symptoms, and as importantly, encouraging patients to become active consumers engaged in trying to find the treatments and resources that help them best.

Lessons Learned About Psychotherapy in Psychosis

The first lesson I learned was in college, in a classroom in 1978: Long term, intensive psychoanalysis cures schizophrenia and other forms of "psychotic denial." It does not merely reduce the severity of symptoms, it cures the illness itself! Most often the focus of treatment was to undo the damage done by the "schizophrenigenic mother" whose style of communicating emotion produced schizophrenia.

The second lesson I learned was years later from the doctor who first diagnosed my brother Henry with schizophrenia: The only treatment for schizophrenia was antipsychotic medication and "supportive therapy." Supportive therapy, at the time, appeared to consist of individual meetings and group therapy aimed at "reality testing" which, to my brother's ears sounded a lot like people telling him he was wrong to think the things he did and was "crazy."

Why the change from psychoanalysis to drugs and reality testing?

A 1984 landmark study conducted by Yale psychiatrist Dr. Tom McGlashan and his colleagues at the Chestnut Lodge, a nationally renowned treatment center for schizophrenia at the time, showed that psychoanalysis by no means cured schizophrenia and in most instances offered very little help at all. Then, in the 1990's, with the National Institute of Mental Health's (NIMH) announcement of the "Decade of the Brain" research initiative for schizophrenia, inspired in large part my family members working with the National Alliance on Mental Illness together with clinicians and scientists, the pendulum swung the other way. Psychotherapy was bad and pharamcotherapy, or drugs, were good. Obviously this is a gross over simplification, but for many of us that was the view. Although I was trained in psychoanalytic psychotherapy and used it with many patients, I saw how antipsychotic medicines were lowering and even

I gladly joined the chorus of well intentioned family members, doctors and researchers who preached that antipsychotic drugs were the key to stabilization and recovery and that there was little or no room for psychotherapy which promised more harm than good. In retrospect, we threw the baby out with the bath water.

eliminating symptoms of schizophrenia in my brother and in others with related psychotic disorders. I gladly joined the chorus of well intentioned family members, doctors and researchers who preached that antipsychotic drugs were the key to stabilization and recovery and that there was little or no room for psychotherapy which promised more harm than good. In retrospect, we threw the baby out with the bath water.

Fortunately, a small group of researchers in the United Kingdom came to the attention of Aaron T. Beck, M.D. from the University of Pennsylvania, the father of cognitive therapy (and my collaborator in the development of an earlier version of LEAP), and together they began a yearly meeting of scientists studying cognitive therapy in patients with and other psychotic disorders. In June of 2009 I attended their 10th anniversary meeting held at the University of Pennsylvania medical school. Although one of my colleagues and I had written a review paper some years before concluding that CBT had many positive applications for persons with schizophrenia and other psychotic disorders, the conference helped to cement and expand this view.[15] Here are some of the lessons I have learned from the conference and the research literature.

The Good Thing about Psychotherapy

First the bad news: The consensus from the conference seemed to be that CBT was not particularly effective in treating negative symptoms. Also, in the USA it is very rarely offered compared to the United Kingdom where it is far more commonplace. The good news is that research conducted since our last review of the literature in 2001 indicates that CBT is effective in treating some positive symptoms of schizophrenia and other psychotic disorders (so called positive symptoms include hallucinations, delusions and thought disorder). Hallucinations, in particular, appear to be helped with CBT.

In our review of the literature in 2001, Dr. Anna Seckinger and I found that poor insight and nonadherence to medication were

---

15. Seckinger, RA, Amador, XF. "Cognitive-behavioral therapy in schizophrenia." *Journal of Psychiatric Practice*, 2001.

common and problematic areas that present major stumbling blocks in the treatment of patients suffering from schizophrenia and other psychotic disorders and that CBT and interventions derived from such approaches, like Motivational Interviewing, improve some aspects of insight into illness, increase adherence to medication, ameliorate the severity of hallucinations and sometimes delusions, and help with other negative consequences of and related psychotic disorders. The papers presented this year at the 10th Anniversary Conference on CBT in Schizophrenia reaffirmed the main findings of our earlier review.

Also, in a study published this year in the British Journal of Psychiatry the authors found that compared to a control therapy, CBT was superior at reducing incidents of aggression–in patients with a history of aggression and violence--and was superior at reducing delusion severity and decreasing risk management. Furthermore, the treatment was acceptable to the majority of individuals; drop out rates from CBT therapy were much lower.

Finally, a review of twenty years of psychosocial research aimed at improving medication adherence, published in the American Journal of Psychiatry in 2002 (*http://leapinstitute. org/RESEARCH.html* and click on "Review Paper") found that only those programs that included elements of Motivational Interviewing were effective in helping motivate persons with schizophrenia to accept treatment and stick with it.

Why Psychotherapy Is Rarely Offered

Despite all the evidence–and even more data for the effectiveness of CBT for treating other disorders common in schizophrenia and related psychotic disorders like mood and anxiety disorders–the overwhelming majority of persons with schizophrenia and related psychotic disorders in North America have never been offered a course of treatment with CBT or related therapies (e.g., LEAP).

I think this is for two reasons. First, there is no schizophrenigenic mother. Unfortunately most clinicians still feel guilt for believing, or being part of a field that once preached that bad parenting caused schizophrenia. To them I say: "Get over it, none of us meant to do any harm, we were simply ignorant and stuck in a particular theory that had never been tested." Second, schizophrenia and related psychotic disorders is indeed a brain disorder.

Consumers, relatives, mental health professionals and policymakers tend to focus first and foremost on the brain, all the while forgetting where the brain resides — in a human being.

The research conducted during the "Decade of the Brain" and after revealed that fact unequivocally. Consequently consumers, relatives, mental health professionals and policymakers tend to focus first and foremost on the brain, all the while forgetting where the brain resides — in a human being. Meanwhile, we have never had a multibillion dollar industry promoting consumer and professional education about psychotherapy for schizophrenia and related psychotic disorders. But we have had such deep pockets educating us about the benefits of antipsychotic medicines. This is not a criticism–it is a simple incontrovertible truth.

So it is up to us to become educated about psychotherapies that have been studied and shown to be effective, and up to us to see that both private and public funds are directed toward training the professionals needed to deliver these therapies and make them available in our communities.[16] I don't find this task daunting or impossible because I have already seen much progress made since I opened my first book about schizophrenia and since my brother's first episode of illness.

---

16. For more information on CBT for persons with schizophrenia and related psychotic disorders see: *www.BeckInstitute.org* and *www.LEAPInstitute.org*

18
Violence and Mental Illness

I woke up searching frantically for my glasses on the night stand-knocking over a glass of water before touching the wire rims. Pulling them on, I saw it was 4 a.m. I was in a cold sweat and my heart was pounding. I could hear Henry pacing in the hallway shouting at the voices only he could hear. The thought to talk with him never entered my mind---I had been up late trying to convince my brother he needed to go back on the medicine, but all I accomplished was to further agitate him. Listening to his side of the heated argument, I started imagining him bursting through the door with a knife in his hand. I couldn't go back to sleep. I swung my legs over the bed and walked to the door with my head hung low in shame and weariness; I locked it.

My research and this book are frequently cited by advocates who promote assisted outpatient treatment (see www.psychlaws. org) and by advocates who oppose involuntary treatments on the grounds they would not be needed if adequate outpatient treatments such as LEAP were available. I can see the wisdom in both sides of the debate. That said, until suicide, gross self-neglect, other forms of self-harm and violence stemming from psychotic states can be reliably controlled, involuntary treatments will always be needed. To turn our heads and look the other way would be immoral and criminal.

Which brings me to the focus of this chapter: Are people with schizophrenia more apt to commit violent crimes and acts compared to "the chronically normal." as my good friend Dr. Fred Freese (a consumer and psychologist with schizophrenia) would say? On a more personal note: Should I have been afraid of my brother who, before he became ill, I trusted more than anyone?

Research on violence and schizophrenia

When giving seminars I often say "Individuals with schizophrenia and related psychotic disorders are no more violent than the general population" and then go on to cite the research that backs me up. For nearly two decades this statement has been a mantra for many of us who are advocates for better treatments, services, and laws for persons with schizophrenia. But more recent, well replicated, research indicates the story is not so simple.

For example, in a recent national study of violent behavior in persons with schizophrenia the authors found that symptoms of losing contact with reality, such as delusions and hallucinations increased the odds of serious violence by nearly three times the normal rate. Results of the study, which was conducted on patients in real-world community settings as part of the NIMH-funded Clinical Antipsychotic Trials of Intervention Effectiveness (CATIE), are consistent with previous independent studies. Most studies show that when hallucinations and delusions are worsened. the potential for violence increases dramatically.

As a forensic expert who has worked on more than 30 death-penalty cases involving persons with schizophrenia and related disorders that have committed homicides, I can say unequivocally that the anecdotal evidence is overwhelming. The story was the same in nearly every case I worked on. When hallucinations, thought disorder, and delusions worsened, the defendants became frightened and angry and, in some cases, coolly planned how they would commit murder. More often than not we are talking about people who became paranoid and/or grandiose, people who, for example, felt convinced they had to defend themselves from their relatives who had become possessed by evil spirits, or accomplish some other delusion-based imperative such as saving the earth from alien invasion by killing a radio talk show host who was broadcasting the beacon the aliens were using to coordinate their attack.

Impaired insight causes medication nonadherence which increases the risk of violence

Most persons with schizophrenia and other psychotic disorders including bipolar disorder, benefit from treatment with antipsychotic medication. When we look at the majority---those who do respond to treatment---we find that the most common cause of medication refusal and partial nonadherence is poor insight. Consequently, if we want to decrease the rate of violence in the population of persons with schizophrenia and other psychotic disorders we have to break the cycle caused by poor insight: Believing "I am not sick" leads to the conclusion, "I don't need medicine" which, in turn, leads to a worsening of those symptoms that cause otherwise-peace-loving people with no history of aggression or violence to become violent.

||||||||||||||||||||||||||||||||||||||||||||||||||||||||||||||||||||||||||||||||||||||||||||||||||||||||||||||||||||||||||||||||||||||||||||

The CATIE study found that participants living with families "they felt listened to them 'most of the time' had half the rate of violence compared to those living with families that did not listen to them."

||||||||||||||||||||||||||||||||||||||||||||||||||||||||||||||||||||||||||||||||||||||||||||||||||||||||||||||||||||||||||||||||||||||||||||

How do we break that cycle? Part of the answer lies in the same nationwide study that recently emphasized the well replicated link between a worsening in psychotic symptoms and violence. The CATIE study found that participants living with families "they felt listened to them 'most of the time' had half the rate of violence compared to those living with families that did not listen to them." If we needed only one reason to try the LEAP Reflective Listening Tool, this would be it.

If they had measured it, I believe the CATIE investigators would have found the same result: less violence in persons working with therapists who listened "most of the time" instead of offering unsolicited advice and debating whether or not their clients were ill. The reason I believe this is because our own research, and that of others, shows that communication strategies that emphasize active listening skills-whether used by therapists, friends, or family, create trusting relationships that lead people to accept treatment even when they do not believe they are ill.

Twenty-five years ago when I was woken from sleep by my brother's rant al his hallucinations, should I have locked the door? In light of the recent research and the professional experiences I have had since that night, I have to say the answer is yes. Although he was never violent, he was nevertheless exhibiting some of the warning signs (increased hallucinations, agitation, and paranoid delusions). At that time, before much of the research on which LEAP is based and the impact of long-acting injectable medications on adherence was completed (see chapter on Treatment above), my only reasonable course of action was to call the police whenever he posed a clear danger to himself and refused treatment. But today when faced with someone who has poor insight into being ill, I often turn first to LEAP and to long-acting injectable medications, to help insure that persons with schizophrenia and related disorders do not experience a worsening of those symptoms that can lead to violence.

Today, when asked "Are people with schizophrenia more violent?" I now answer "No. Not when they are in treatment and the symptoms are well controlled."

19
DSM-V and Anosognosia

The *Diagnostic and Statistical Manual for Mental Disorders, 5th Edition (DSM-V)* is in the works and will likely be published about 2012. Over the last twenty years I worked on the last two editions as a *Schizophrenia Expert, Columbia University Field Trial Coordinator*, a couple of other roles and most recently as the *co-chair of the Schizophrenia and Related Disorders* section. My co-chair, Michael Flaum, MD, and I were asked by the American Psychiatric Association (APA) to revise the text to insure that it was based on scientific consensus rather than on the views of a single expert.

To accomplish this we brought together experts from around the United States and overseas to read the research and independently review the text we proposed so that it would accurately reflect the scientific evidence available at the time. After our text revision (TR) and peer review process, the text was independently reviewed again by experts on the APA Task Force for the *DSM-V-TR*.

At that time (10 years ago), our peer-reviewers and the APA Task Force agreed that *"a majority of individuals with schizophrenia lacked insight into having a psychotic illness" and that this problem was "a manifestation of the illness itself rather than a coping strategy"* (page 304, *DSM-IV-TR*, APA Press, 2000). It was a symptom of the brain disorder rather than denial. It was compared to anosognosia-an unawareness syndrome seen in stroke patients and others with frontal lobe lesions.

I realize I have quoted this passage from the latest DSM several times in this 10th Anniversary edition of *I am Not*

Sick, I Don't Need Help! The reason is that after ten years most psychiatrists and other mental health professionals continue to feel certain that what they are dealing with—when a patient says "I am not sick"over a period of months, years and decades--is denial. They have never read the passage or if they have, they have not read the underlying research. They hold on to the belief that the poor insight they see is denial rather than a symptom of the disorder, rather than brain dysfunction. So please forgive me for being redundant.

I speak frequently all over the United States and overseas and for the past ten years I have been asking my audiences if they have heard of anosognosia and whether they believe this unawareness syndrome exists in schizophrenia and related disorders (e.g. schizoaffective disorder and other psychotic illnesses). In the early years, only one or two hands went up on groups of two hundred or more. Today, between one-half to two-thirds of my audiences raise their hands whether in Australia, New Zealand, France, Belgium, Hawaii, Hungary, Spain or Ohio (and nearly every other U.S. State).

However, many mental health professionals and family members still have trouble believing it. For this reason-because of the continuing gap between science and practice-I will briefly review the research that has convinced me and most other experts on schizophrenia that when a patient (who has received a reliable diagnosis) with this disorder persists for years in saying "I am not sick, I don't need help!" he is giving voice to a symptom of the illness (similar to a delusion) rather than to denial.

Studies using neuropsychological tests

Numerous studies consistently report that low performance on the Wisconsin Card Sorting Test (WCST) is significantly correlated with insight deficits in patients with schizophrenia (e.g. Shad et. al., 2006; see also the relevant review chapter in

Amador and David, *Insight and Psychosis*, edited volume, Oxford University Press, 2004). The WCST measures, among other things, executive functions (anterior cortical function, a.k.a. frontal lobe function) such as self-reflection, planning, rule acquisition, abstract thinking initiating appropriate actions while inhibiting inappropriate actions. Frontal lobe lesions have been found to be a common cause of anosognosia in neurological disorders (see reviews in: Amador et. al., *Schizophrenia Bulletin*, 1991 and in Amador, X. *I am Not Sick, I Don't Need Help!* (Vida Press, 2007).

Structural brain imaging studies

Although far fewer in number, studies of the neurobiological underpinnings of poor insight in schizophrenia generally find that anosognosia in schizophrenia is correlated with a range of frontal lobe abnormalities (see: Alexander and Struss, 2006; see also the relevant review chapter in: Amador and David, Insight and Psychosis, edited volume, Oxford University Press, 2004).

Additional structural and functional brain imaging studies and post-mortem brain studies are currently underway and should help to shed light on the pathophysiology of this common symptom of schizophrenia.

How research should influence the DSM-V

Psychiatric diagnoses are purely descriptive. To date, there is no blood test or brain scan that can diagnose mental illness. We look instead for diagnostic categories and dimensions that tell us something about what is likely to happen to the person (i.e. we ask, "What is the predictive value or validity of the diagnostic category or subtype?"). This also helps us to choose and recommend treatments and services that will be helpful to the individual. The current subtypes of schizophrenia (e.g. catatonic, undifferentiated, disorganized, etc.) have limited predictive value. For that reason—and because the extensive research on poor insight in schizophrenia indicates that patients with this symptom have a poorer course of illness, are more prone to violence, homelessness, and poor adherence to treatments – the time to use the level of "awareness of illness" as a subtype and/or dimension in the DSM is long overdue. This is especially true when we look at the research on motivational enhancement therapy (MET), or Motivational Interviewing, and cognitive behavioral therapy (CBT) which, along with long-acting injectable medications, are clearly the treatments of choice for such individuals. When a psychiatrist or other mental health professional meets someone with schizophrenia and does the initial evaluation, the question of whether the individual is like half of all persons with schizophrenia and related disorders who do not understand they are ill and, as a consequence, refuse treatment and services, should always be asked.

The first step after making a diagnosis is to... and identify whether the person...has anosognosia. Once we do that, we can then choose a different path toward stabilization and recovery-one that employs science-proven communication skills and medications designed to help persons with poor insight and poor adherence to treatment.

Such patients fight with well-meaning clinicians and family members who are trying to engage them in the interventions that can give them a chance at recovery. They (understandably, because they are certain nothing is wrong with them) toss out prescriptions, appointment cards, and advice regarding their disorder and treatments. We know how to engage such persons in treatment – the science exists. The first step after making a diagnosis is to do a careful assessment of insight into illness and identify whether the person being evaluated has anosognosia. Once we do that, we can then choose a different path toward stabilization and recovery-one that employs science-proven communication skills and medications designed to help persons with poor insight and poor adherence to treatment.

20
Henry

On April 23, 2007, while helping a woman put her groceries on a bus, my brother Henry was hit by a car while standing on a sidewalk and died at the scene. He had stepped off the bus and back on to the sidewalk to help the woman he saw was struggling with her groceries. There's actually a videotape, taken by the bus company, of what he did though I don't yet have the strength to watch it. That was so like him. Although often lost in delusional thoughts and distracted by hallucinations, he was aware of people around him, especially those in need, and cared.

That was not what he or I had planned for. When I first wrote about this, only two months after his death, I was much too close to my loss and mourning to know what good could possibly come from this, I trusted that someday something would.

Saying Goodbye Twice

Standing at the lectern looking out at the people who had come to Henry's funeral, I was struck once again by what a full life he had. His friends filled the church, prompting several of my family members---who had very little contact with Henry after he became ill 25 years before—to say things like "I had no idea he had this many friends!" and "I never knew his life was so full."

As they met and spoke to more and more of his friends over the course of that day and the next, some in my family expressed deep remorse and sadness that they had missed out on so much of his life. I didn't feel that sadness because I had not missed out. My brother and I were very close and loved each other's company immensely.

He was my hero.

The reason I had this relationship with Henry while others in our family did not is not because I am a better person; I am no saint. The reason is that after he first became ill, I was somehow able to mourn who he had been before, while most of my brothers and sisters (there are nine of us) seemed unable to. At first, I know we all felt it...it was impossible to accept that he was no longer there in the way he had been and that could never become the man we all had envisioned he would be: a loving husband and father, a responsible care giver and successful man.

He was handsome, kind, and loving. He had a magical sense of humor.

When he became ill with schizophrenia we all longed for the "old Henry" and made little room in our hearts for the "new Henry."

He had the same problem.

For the first five years of his illness he, like us, was stuck on the plan he had had for the future, and he became depressed that what he had planned for mow seemed impossible to attain. Prior to becoming ill he had always worked, gone to university and had girlfriends. That was over now. Not until he had mourned his old vision for the future did he discover that the core of the old Henry was still there. He realized that new plans needed to be made.

The last year of his life he was especially happy. This is not some wishful revisionist delusion on my part – it is confirmed by all that were close to him. He had many friends; he worked odd jobs with his friend "Pops," and his girlfriend Mary had become a big part of his life.

Mourning when mental illness strikes

The research is clear on the importance of mourning. By mourning what has been lost, you open your eyes to all that is still there. Moreover, you open your eyes and heart to new possibilities.

In a review of the research on literature we published in the spring of 2007 in the *Annals of General Psychiatry*, my colleagues and I found that people with schizophrenia who had successfully mourned were less likely to feel suicidal. Studies of family members of people with schizophrenia have found that those relatives that who have mourned the loss of the way things used to be are less likely to be critical of their mentally ill loved ones, and feel less burdened and stressed.

Some research findings are intuitive; they just make sense. This is one of those instances. I've seen the same transformation in my brother and I experienced the improvement in his hopefulness about his future and our relationship. I've seen this repeated time and again in patients and families I have worked with this last 25 years.

Closing one door opens another

It is like any other major change in life. When you mourn, you feel sad because you are saying goodbye to what was and what you hoped would be. But by doing this, you feel at peace and even happy as you say hello to what is and what can be. I have counseled many families and also consumers on the importance of going through this process. Families that successfully mourn are able to let go of their anger at their loved ones. They have learned to separate the illness from the person. Communication gets healthier, and even the course of illness can improve because of the lessened tensions between family members. But I never before experienced the stark truth of this wisdom so completely as I did when my brother died. Now that he is gone, I find I have no regrets. I cherish countless good memories I have of him. I recall our many conversations and how often he would ramble and it would be hard for me to listen, but he would always end by saying. "You're my baby brother, I love you." I remember our nearly constant laughter together, his helping me build an outdoor fireplace in my home which crackled with flame and heat for my family earlier this evening, his giving me permission to write about him, the pride he felt in me and I in him and so much more.

After Henry became ill, many things changed. But not the fact that he was still smart, handsome, kind, and loving. And he could make me laugh in any situation—I am talking about the splitting-your-gut kind of laughter, even at our mother's funeral! But usually with kindness and reverence for the feelings of other people—except for those rare instances later in life when the illness got the best of him. Because he felt less inhibited, he was far funnier than he was prior to becoming ill and he knew it.

Many people have written to me to offer their condolences, to share their good memories of Henry, and to wisely say how lucky I was to have him as my older brother. They are right. But they left out one vital thing, a lesson I learned anew as I reflect on the seemingly insurmountable task of saying goodbye to him all over again: I was especially fortunate that I was able to mourn after he first became ill—to say goodbye to what I had hoped for—so that these past 25 years I could laugh with him, make new good memories together, and realize just how lucky I was to be his "baby brother." He worked with me to get well and our relationship was a good one. He helped many people through his example, influence on my thinking and willingness to let his story be told in my books and articles. We will never know how many lives he saved and how many people with poor insight he helped to recover. I have received many letters from kind souls telling me he had that impact. I am sure there are many more who have not written.

I have much to be grateful for.

Acknowledgments

I am grateful, first and foremost to my daughter, Lou-Andréa. Thank you for your love, patience and sacrifice while I revised this book. Thank you most for making me laugh even when I was "grumpy man" and for making me feel like the luckiest man on earth. Thanks for "Papi's the man" and for insisting I not shave. I love you more than you can know.

My thanks also to Bob and Jason for your support and help while writing this book and with our other work together. Thanks to Dr. Dave Schaich for pitching in and giving LEAP seminars when I could not.

Since the publication of the first edition of this book I have given lectures to tens of thousands of family members, mental health professionals, consumers, attorneys and judges the U.S., Canada, and overseas. The response to the message and lessons in this book has been truly overwhelming. With each invitation to speak and every e-mail and phone call I receive, I am reminded again that I am bound to my readers by much more than a book. The shared experiences, words of appreciation, and lessons I have learned from these contacts have been invaluable and inspired me to write this 10th anniversary edition.

Once again, I especially want to thank the many people with mental illness who have opened up to me over the past twenty-five years and taught me about their experience. Thanks also to the students I have supervised. Without their enthusiasm for understanding the people whose care they were entrusted with, I would never have had to translate research findings into practical advice they could use in their clinical work.

Many organizations have supported the research described in this book. I want to thank them for their support and for their commitment to research on serious mental illness. My thanks to the National Alliance for Research on Schizophrenia and Affective

Disorders (NARSAD), the Stanley Research Foundation, the Scottish Rite Foundation, the National Institute of Mental Health (NIMH), and the National Alliance on Mental Illness (NAMI).

And once again, *muchos gracias a mi hermano.* Thank you for letting me tell our story and for being the kindest and most supportive older brother a person could ask for. Your perseverance and sense of humor set a standard I continue to strive to meet. I miss you despite feeling your presence every day.

Xavier Amador, October 6, 2009 (Henry's birthday)

NB: Mercí, Daniel, for your blunt honesty and editorial advice. I think the acknowledgments would now meet with your approval.

Literature cited

Amador XF, Flaum M, Andreasen NC, Strauss DH, Yale SA, ClarkSC, & Gorman JM. Awareness of illness in schizophrenia and schizoaffective and mood disorders. *Archives of General Psychiatry*, 51:826-836. 1994.

Amador XF & David AS (Eds.) *Insight and Psychosis. Awareness of Illness in Schizophrenia and Related Disorders.* Oxford University Press, 2005.

Amador XF & Gorman JM. "Psychopathologic domains and insight in schizophrenia." *Psychiatric Clinics of North America*, 20:27-42, 1998.

Amador XF, "Closing the Gap between Science and Practice," *Civil Rights Law Journal*, in press.

AmadorXF, Strauss DH, Yale SA, Flaum M, Endicott J, & Gorman JM. Assessment of Insight in Psychosis. *American Journal of Psychiatry*, 150:873-879. 1993.

Amador XF, Barr W.B.; Economou, A.; Mallin, E.; Marcinko, L.; Yale, S."Awareness deficits in neurological disorders and schizophrenia."*Schizophrenia Research*, 24(1-2): 96-97, 1997.

Amador XF, Harkavy Friedman J, Kasapis C, Yale SA, Flaum M, & Gorman JM. "Suicidal behavior and its relationship to awareness of illness." *American Journal of Psychiatry*, 153:1185-1188, 1996.

Amador XF & Seckinger RA. "The assessment of insight." *Psychiatric Annals*, 27(12):798-805, 1997.

Amador XF & Strauss DH. Poor insight in schizophrenia. *Psychiatric Quarterly*, 64:305-318. 1993.

Amador XF; Strauss DH; Yale SA & Gorman JM. Awareness of Illness in Schizophrenia. *Schizophrenia Bulletin,* 17:113-132, 1991.

Bartko G., Herczog I. & Zador G. Clinical symptomatology and drug compliance in schizophrenic patients. *Acta Psychiatrica Scandinavica,* 77:74-76. 1988.

McEvoy JP, Applebaum PS, Geller JL, Freter S. Why must some schizophrenic patients be involuntarily committed?The role of insight. *Comprehensive Psychiatry,* 30:13-17. 1989.

Bartko G; Herczog I & Zador G.Clinical Symptomatology and Drug Compliance in Schizophrenic Patients.*Acta Psychiatrica Scandinavica,* 77:74-76, 1988.

Caracci G; Mukherjee S; Roth S & Decina P.Subjective Awareness of Abnormal Involuntary Movements in Chronic Schizophrenic Patients. *American Journal of Psychiatry,* 147:295-298. 1990.

Cuesta MJ & Peralta V. Lack of Insight in Schizophrenia.*Schizophrenia Bulletin,* 20:359-366. 1994.

Flashman LA,McAllister TW,Saykin AJ, Johnson SC, Rick JH,Green RL, Neuroanatomical Correlates of Unawareness of Illness in Schizophrenia. From the Neuropsychology & Brain Imaging Laboratories, Dept. of Psychiatry, Dartmouth Medical School, Lebanon, NH & New Hampshire Hospital, Concord, NH 03301. Presented at the *Biennial Meeting of the International Congress on Schizophrenia Research,* Santa Fe, New Mexico, April 20, 1999

Ghaemi NS & Pope HG, Jr.Lack of Insight in Psychotic and Affective Disorders : A Review of Empirical Studies.*Harvard Review of Psychiatry,* May/June: 22-33. 1994.

Greenfield D; Strauss JS; Bowers MB & Mandelkern M.Insight and Interpretation of Illness in Recovery from Psychosis.*Schizophrenia Bulletin*, 15:245-252. 1989.

Heinrichs DW; Cohen BP & Carpenter WT, Jr.Early Insight and the Management of Schizophrenic Decompensation. Journal of Nervous and Mental Disease, 173:133-138. 1985.

Kampman O.Lehtinen K. Compliance in psychoses.*Acta Psychiatrica Scandinavica*. 100(3):167-75, 1999

Lysaker PH; Bell MD; Milstein R; Bryson G & Beam Goulet J.Insight and Psychosocial Treatment Compliance in Schizophrenia.*Psychiatry*, Vol. 57. 1994.

Lysaker PH. Bell MD. Bryson G. Kaplan E.Neurocognitive function and insight in schizophrenia: support for an association with impairmentsin executive function but not with impairments in global function.*Acta Psychiatrica Scandinavica*. 97(4):297-301, 1998

McEvoy JP; Appelbaum PS; Geller JL & Freter S.Why Must Some Schizophrenic Patients be Involuntarily Committed ? The Role of Insight.*Comprehensive Psychiatry* 30:13-17. 1989.

McEvoy JP, Apperson LJ, Applebaum PS, Ortlip P, Brecosky J, Hammill K.Insight in schizophrenia.Its relationship to acute psychopathology. *Journal of Nervous and Mental Disorders*, 177:43-47. 1989.

McGlashan TH; Levy ST & Carpenter WT, Jr.Integration and Sealing Over: Clinically Distinct Recovery Styles from Schizophrenia.*Archives of General Psychiatry*, 32:1269-1272, 1975.

McGlashan TH & Carpenter WT Jr..Does attitude toward psychosis relate to outcome? *American Journal of Psychiatry*, 138:797-801. 1981.

Michalakeas A; Skoutas C; Charalambous A; Peristeris A; Marinos V; Keramari E & Theologou A. Insight in Schizophrenia and Mood Disorders and its Relation to Psychopathology.*Acta Psychiatrica Scandinavica*, 90:46-49, 1994.

Mohamed S. Fleming S. Penn DL. Spaulding W. Insight in schizophrenia: its relationshipto measures of executive functions. *Journal of Nervous & Mental Disease*. 187(9):525-31, 1999

Morgan KD, Vearnals S, Hutchinson G, Orr KGD, Greenwood K, Sharpley R, Mallet R, Morris R, David A, Leff J, Murray RM. Insight, ethnicity, and neuropsychology in first-onset psychosis. *Schizophrenia Research*, 36(1-3): 144. 1999.

Morgan KD, Orr KGD, Hutchinson G, Vearnals S, Greenwood K, Sharpley M, Mallet R, Morris R, David A, Lefef J, Murray RM.Insight and neuropsychology in first-onset schizophrenia and other psychoses. *Schizophrenia Research*, 36(1-3): 145. 1999.

Smith TE. Hull JW. Santos L. The relationship between symptoms and insight in schizophrenia: a longitudinal perspective.*Schizophrenia Research*. 33(1-2):63-7, 1998.

Swanson Cl, Jr.; Freudenreich O; McEvoy JP; Nelson L; Kamaraju L & Wilson WH.Insight in Schizophrenia and Mania.*The Journal of Nervous and Mental Disease*, 183:752-755, 1995.

Takai A, Uematsu M, Ueki H, Sone K and Kaiya Hisanobu.Insight and its Related Factors in ChronicSchizophrenic Patients: A preliminary Study.*European Journal of Psychiatry*, 6:159-170, 1992.

Voruganti LN. Heslegrave RJ. Awad AG. Neurocognitive correlates of positive and negative syndromes inschizophrenia.*Canadian Journal of Psychiatry.* 42(10):1066-71, 1997.

Wciorka J.A Clinical Typology of Schizophrenic PatientsAttitudes towards their Illness. *Psychopathology,* 21:259-266, 1988.

Wilson WH,Ban T & Guy W.. Flexible System Criteria in Chronic Schizophrenia. *Comprehensive Psychiatry,* 27:259-265. 1986.

World Health Organization. Report of the International Pilot Study of Schizophrenia. Geneva: World Health Organization Press. 1973.

Young et al. Medication adherence failure in schizophrenia: a forensic review of rates, reasons, treatments, and prospects.*Journal of the American Academy of Psychiatry and the Law,* 1999;27(3):426-44.

Young DA, Davila R, Scher H..Unawareness of illness and neuropsychological performance in chronic schizophrenia.*Schizophrenia Research,* 10:117-124. 1993.

Young DA, Zakzanis KK, Baily C, Davila R, Griese J, Sartory G& Thom A. Further Parameters of Insight and Neuropsychological Deficit in Schizophrenia and Other Chronic Mental Disease.*Journal of Nervous and Mental Disease,* 186: 44-50. 1998.

Research on Cognitive Therapy for Schizophrenia

Kemp R, Hayward P, Applewhaite G, Everitt B, David A: Compliance therapy in psychotic patients: a randomized controlled trial. BMJ 1996; 312:345–349

Kemp R, Kirov G, Everitt B, Hayward P, David A: Randomized controlled trial of compliance therapy: 18 month follow-up. Br J Psychiatry 1998; 172:413–419

Kline N, Li C, Lehmann H, Lajtha A, Laski E, Cooper T: Beta-endorphin-induced changes in schizophrenic and depressed patients. Arch Gen Psychiatry 1977; 34:1111–1113

McGorry PD, Yung AR, Phillips LJ, Yuen HP, Francey S, Cosgrave EM, Germano D, Bravin J, McDonald T, Blair A, Adlard S, Jackson H: Randomized controlled trial of interventions designed to reduce the risk of progression to first-episode psychosis in a clinical sample with subthreshold symptoms. Arch Gen Psychiatry 2002; 59:921–928

Mosher LR, Menn AZ: Community residential treatment for schizophrenia: a two-year follow-up. Hosp Community Psychiatry 1978; 29:715–723

O'Donnell C, Donohoe G, Sharkey L, Owens N, Migone M, Harries R, Kinsella A, Larkin C, O'Callaghan E: Compliance therapy: a randomised controlled trial in schizophrenia. BMJ 2003; 327:834

Sensky T, Turkington D, Kingdon D, Scott JL, Scot J, Siddle R, O'Carroll M, Barnes TRE: A randomized controlled trial of cognitive-behavioral therapy for persistent symptoms of schizophrenia resistant to medication. Arch Gen Psychiatry 2000; 57:165–172

Tarrier N, Yusupoff L, Kinney C, McCarthy C, Gledhill A, Haddock G, Morris J: Randomised controlled trial of intensive cognitive behaviour therapy for patients with chronic schizophrenia. BMJ 1998; 317:303–307

Tarrier N, Wittkowski A, Kinney C, McCarthy C, Morris J, Humphreys L: Durability of the effects of cognitive-behavioural therapy in the treatment of schizophrenia: 12-month follow-up. Br J Psychiatry 1999; 174:500–504

Tarrier N, Kinney C, McCarthy E, Humphreys L, Wittkowski A, Morris J: Two-year follow-up of cognitive-behavioral therapy and supportive counseling in the treatment of persistent symptoms in chronic schizophrenia. J Consult Clin Psychol 2000; 68:917–922

Wagemaker H Jr, Cade R: The use of hemodialysis in chronic schizophrenia. Am J Psychiatry 1977; 134:684–685

Recommended Books

Surviving Schizophrenia (fourth Edition) by E. Fuller Torrey. HarperCollins, 2001

Crazy. A Father's Search through America's Mental Health Madness. Putnam, 2006

Insight and Psychosis. Awareness of Illness in Schizophrenia and Related Disorders. Amador XF & David AS (Eds.) Oxford University Press, 2005

Cognitive-Behavioral Therapy of Schizophrenia by David G. Kingdon and Douglas Turkington. The Guilford Press, 1993_

When Someone You Love is Depressed. How to Help without losing yourself. Laura Epstein and Xavier Amador. Fireside, 1998

The Day the Voices Stopped. A Memoir of Madness and Hope. Ken Steele and Claire Berman. Basic Books, 2001

Recommended Resources

Advocacy & Professional Organizations

National Alliance on Mental Illness (NAMI)
www.NAMI.org
Colonial Place Three
2107 Wilson Blvd., Suite 300
Arlington, VA 22201-3042
Main: (703) 524-7600
Fax: (703) 524-9094
Member Services: (800) 950-NAMI

In my experience, NAMI is probably the best source for support and information about serious mental illness. It was founded in 1979 by families of mentally ill people who were frustrated by the lack of services, treatment, research, and education available for mentally ill people and their relatives. It has become an influential and important advocacy group with local chapters in almost every major city as well as many smaller towns. Many chapters offer free "Family-to-Family," "In Our Own Voices" and, "Peer-to-Peer" programs that I highly recommend. Some chapters have hotlines you can call during a crisis or just to get information about services in your area. NAMI also offers excellent books and pamphlets about mental illness.

The National Mental Health Association (NMHA)
www.NMHA.org
National Mental Health Association
2001 N. Beauregard Street, 12th Floor
Alexandria, Virginia 22311
Main : (703) 684-7722
Toll-free: (800) 969-NMHA (6642)

The National Mental Health Association is another effective nonprofit organization that addresses many aspects of mental health and mental illness. With more than 340 affiliates nationwide, NMHA works to improve the mental health of all Americans, especially the 54 million people with mental disorders, through advocacy, education, research, and service.

National Alliance for Research on Schizophrenia and Depression (NARSAD)
www.NARSAD.org
60 Cutter Mill Road
Suite 404
Great Neck, NY 11021
Tel: 516-829-0091 and 800-829-8292

NARSAD, also a nonprofit organization, was established to raise money for research into affective disorders and schizophrenia. It has been immensely successful in funding promising new scientists and supporting the research of more senior investigators. NARSAD-supported scientists have conducted many landmark studies over the past decade. NARSAD raises more money yearly for psychiatric research than any other organization of its kind. Its free newsletter is a wonderful source of up-to-date information on new research.

Depression and Bipolar Support Alliance (DBSA)
www.dbsalliance.org
730 North Franklin Street
Suite 501
Chicago, IL 60610
Phone: (800) 826-3632

The DBSA consists of people with clinical depression and their families who try to educate the public about depression and manic-depression and help others find treatment. The central branch responds to requests for referrals in other areas of the country and can refer you to local qualified mental health professionals. If you contact them, you should also consider inquiring about their quarterly newsletter, which provides up-to-date information and research findings about depression and manic-depression. The newsletter is free with membership in the association.

Depression Awareness, Recognition, and Treatment (D/ART)
National Institute of Mental Health,
5600 Fishers Lane
Room 10-85
Rockville, MD
Phone: (800) 421-4211

This organization can give you good general information about depression, its signs and symptoms, and the latest in treatment options. D/ART publishes some excellent booklets and brochures about depression that you can request.

American Association of Suicidology
2459 South Ash
Denver, CO 80222
Phone: (303) 692-0985

This organization offers a variety of printed suicide prevention materials, primarily for use in schools and other institutional settings. However, they can also refer you to suicide hotlines and support groups in your area.

American Psychological Association
750 1st Street, N.E., Washington, D.C. 20002
Phone: (202) 336-5500

American Psychiatric Association
1400 K Street, N.W., Washington, D.C. 20005
Phone: (202) 682-6066

These last two organizations are the national associations of the professions of psychology and psychiatry, respectively. If you contact them, they can send you information about serious mental illnesses and their treatment, as well as refer you their qualified members in your area. The American Psychological Association also publishes fact sheets (*Facts About Manic Depression, Facts About Schizophrenia,* etc.) that are very informative.

Informative Websites

Treatment Advocacy Center
www.psychlaws.org.

The National Institute on Mental Health
www.NIMH.org

www.Schizophrenia.com.
www.reintegration.com
www.schizophreniadigest.com
www.bipolarmagazine.com
www.bipolar.com

Praise for the first edition

I am Not Sick, I Don't Need Help!
Helping the Seriously Mentally Ill Accept Treatment.

At last we have a volume for those individuals most closely associated with the mentally ill. In a very readable fashion, Dr. Amador addresses the nature of patients' unawareness of their illness and their need for treatment. He also clearly outlines the relevant research and gives clear prescriptions to help families and therapists deal with patients' obliviousness to their condition. I strongly recommend this to families and therapists of individuals with serious mental illness.

AARON T. BECK, M.D., *Emeritus Professor of Psychiatry, University of Pennsylvania, Department of Psychiatry*

This is the first book to address the elephantine question running roughshod over families of individuals with schizophrenia and bipolar disorder: *Why won't the sick person take his/her medicine?* Amador, a psychologist who has a brother with schizophrenia, has pioneered research on poor insight into illness, a.k.a. anosognosia, for the past decade and is an acknowledged authority on it. He blends clinical vignettes skillfully with his erudition, and the resulting mix is both edible and edifying. Most important, Amador provides families and mental health professionals with a concrete, step-by-step plan to improve awareness of illness. This book fills a tremendous void in the literature on schizophrenia and bipolar disorder.

E. FULLER TORREY, M.D., *Author of* Surviving Schizophrenia

Looking back, the strangest part was not the omnipresent government agents, the agonizing radiation weapons, or even my own super hero-like capabilities. What frightens me most is that my manic depression gave me an immovable certainty that it was the world around me that was convulsing but that my perception and judgment of it were unaltered. Thinking of this time leaves me frustrated and embarrassed as well as apprehensive that it might come again. I read Dr. Amador's book and felt better. First, he concretely and understandably establishes that most denials of treatment are but manifestations of the illness and that it is the illness that is the enemy. Dr. Amador then presents a powerful game plan for penetrating, or at least circumventing, sickness induced lack of insight that will maximize the cooperation with treatment of those affected. When I first became ill, I wish this book had been in the hands of someone who cared about me.

JONATHAN STANLEY, JD, *Assistant Director, Treatment Advocacy Center and a Consumer diagnosed with Bipolar Disorder*

There are several publications that address best practices for clinicians treating persons with schizophrenia. These are written from the perspective of the practitioner. There are a few books written from the perspective of the consumer or of the family member, but these do not incorporate the values of clinical insights, particularly those reflecting recent research findings. The great value of "I am Not Sick, I Don't Need Help" is that it incorporates both the consumer's perspective and that of the clinician. It finds common ground, pointing out where the consumer and his/her clinician can work together in partnership. It is practical, easy to read, and hopeful. I highly recommend it to anyone interested in helping those who, like myself, live with the condition we call schizophrenia.

FREDERIC J. FRESE III, Ph.D., *Summit County Recovery Project and a Consumer diagnosed with Schizophrenia*

Of the myriad of problems presented by serious mental illness Dr. Amador has focused on the single most critical factor. Breakthroughs in treatment will not be effective unless we deal with medication noncompliance and the related issue of poor insight into illness. Dr. Amador takes this issue on in "I am Not Sick I Don't Need Help" and deals with it head-on, providing vital information and practical advice for both families and therapists of patients with schizophrenia and bipolar disorder. This book will be immensely helpful to anyone dealing with the problems of medication noncompliance and poor insight.

MICHAEL FLAUM, M.D., *Director of Mental Health, State of Iowa*

This is a wonderful book bringing together the personal experiences of a psychologist and a lay person who have relatives with serious mental illness. Dr. Amador's research and clinical experience makes this book a rich source of information and practical advice. It is one of the salutary characteristics of our culture that people who experience pain convert that pain into something productive. People who are victimized by, stressed by, and dismayed by serious mental illness will find this book enormously helpful. It contains information about new research and concrete advice that will be of enormous help to both the families of the seriously mentally ill and to the mental health professionals who care for them.

HERBERT PARDES, M.D., *President, New York-Presbyterian, The University Hospital of Columbia and Cornell, and past Director of the National Institute of Mental Health*

"I am Not Sick, I Don't Need Help!" is essential reading material for family members battling with their mentally ill loved ones about the need for treatment. Dr. Amador provides an insightful, compassionate, and practical guide for handling the frustration and guilt that inevitably arises when dealing with a sick individual who, by virtue of their illness, is completely unaware of the need for treatment. What makes this book especially poignant is Dr. Amador's inclusion of his own personal account of his lifelong struggle with his own brother who suffers from schizophrenia, as well as his detailed presentations of patient cases. He does an exceptional job summarizing the compelling science behind poor insight, or anosognosia, clarifying that the loved one's lack of insight is not a product of a psychological defense mechanism, but is a result of the very brain dysfunction that underlies the illness. Practical tips on how to help a loved one with poor insight accept treatment or how to proceed with civil commitment, if necessary, make this book especially useful.

MICHAEL B. FIRST, M.D., *Editor,* Diagnostic and Statistical Manual of Mental Disorders, Fourth Edition (DSM-IV)

This is a well-written and must-read practical guide for those facing serious mental illness in a loved one, friend, or colleague. Delusions and psychotic thinking are quite beyond our everyday experiences, so it is not surprising that most people are at a loss about how to approach and obtain help for someone with serious mental illness. Those with psychosis may not even recognize that their own behavior and function is disturbed, let alone that they need treatment. If only the ailment were a stomachache rather than a malady in the part of the brain that distinguishes normal from abnormal!

DOLORES MALASPINA, M.D., *Professor of Psychiatry, Columbia University College of Physicians and Surgeons and Director, Clinical Neurobiology in Medical Genetics*

Lack of insight in people with schizophrenia and bipolar disorder is the major cause of many of the worst aspects of their illness, and may be the most recalcitrant since it is difficult to treat someone who thinks that nothing is wrong. Dr. Amador has spent the better part of two decades conducting research on this topic and has been the world's most influential scientist in this important area of work. In this book, he prescribes detailed interventions to help families and therapists deal with lack of insight and the many difficulties it causes people with major mental illness. Yet Amador is not an academic preaching from an ivory tower. His poignant personal experiences with people with schizophrenia, including his brother and close friend, are laced throughout this thoughtful, moving, and indispensable book. "I am Not Sick, I Don't Need Help!" is an essential guide to anyone who knows, loves or treats someone with schizophrenia or bipolar disorder.

RICHARD KEEFE, PH.D., *Professor of Psychology in Psychiatry, Duke University Medical Center and author of* Understanding Schizophrenia

It is uncommon to find books that bring together the latest findings in psychiatry research with relevant and practical clinical advice. Even less common are those that do so in a readable and engaging fashion, for both families and mental health professionals. Dr. Amador accomplishes all of the above in "I am Not Sick I Don't Need Help!"

ROBERTO GIL, M.D., *Director, Schizophrenia Research Unit at Columbia University and the New York State Psychiatric Institute.*

There is probably no more difficult or more important responsibility for a family member in our society than meeting the needs of a mentally ill child, sibling or close relative. Daily life can be a struggle and the future impenetrable with uncertainty. Dr. Amador has taken up the challenge of guiding the family member in order to bring a better life to the afflicted patient and the responsible relatives. The unique combination of sensitivities he brings to this task reflect both his life experience as a sibling of an afflicted brother and his many years of broad clinical practice.

Reflecting his own profound empathy and insight, the book is a guide to the shocked, bewildered and too often hopeless close relative. It is no mere compendium of generalizations.It is a practical, step-by-step, program for achieving understanding and even expressing love in a situation where that love is difficult to convey.

His is a remarkable achievement and a great public service. Many lives of patients and their loved ones could be enhanced, often immeasurably if copies of this book were given to the families of every patient who begins to show signs of psychosis.As people use this book, it will mark the beginning of a sound remediation and even rehabilitation.

CONNIE LIEBER, *President, National Alliance for Research on Schizophrenia and Depression*

I'm Not Sick,I Don't Need Help! addresses one of the toughest and most emotional problems in delivering mental health services. Dr. Xavier Amador and Anna-Lisa Johanson tackle this challenge by drawing ontheir own painful personalexperience.The book offers a sensitive presentation of a practical, clinically sound, approach to getting a severely ill personto accept needed treatment.

Written in a respectful tone, the book provides clear, concrete guidance to families and professionals.Skillful use of case examples enlivens the text, which is filled with difficult "real world" situations. The focus throughout is on building mutual understanding and trust, so involuntary treatment can be avoided, if possible.

I hope this book will be widely read.It gives us amuch-needed and long overdue common ground for helping people in crisis.

LAURIE FLYNN, *Former Executive Director, National Alliance for the Mentally Ill (NAMI)*

I hope you will be as impressed as I am with this book's approach to treatment for persons with serious mental illness. I strongly applaud Dr. Amador for working out these treatment strategies and for the sage advice he gives for persons involved in what continues to be one of the most challenging and perplexing arenas in modern health care.

In this book, Dr. Amador lays out a specific plan of attack that addresses this difficult problem. It is an effective strategy for finding common ground that can be used to build trust and cooperation for mutually addressing the problems of the patient. The justification and description of the "listen-empathize-agree-partnership" approach rings true to this person who "has been there." Particularly valuable is the recommendation that clinicians and relatives not openly challenge the beliefs of the mentally ill person. Unfortunately such challenging is still quite common and is frequently justified by the thought that "you should not buy into the belief system" of a delusional person. Such thinking among mental health providers is misguided. What is important, particularly during the initial stages of interaction is that the professional afford dignity to those in his care. How important it is to communicate respect.

In addition to describing effective strategies for dealing with mentally ill persons and providing a list of helpful resources, Dr. Amador provides delightful anecdotes that emphasize his main points and illustrate his suggestions. These serve as excellent mechanisms for tying his recommendations to the realities of trying to help mentally ill persons.

FREDERIC J. FRESE III, PH.D., *Clinical Assistant Professor of Psychology in Psychiatry, Northeast Ohio Universities College of Medicine and a Consumer diagnosed with Schizophrenia*

LEAP
QUICK START GUIDE

‖‖‖

LISTEN
Reflectively
to:

Delusions
Anosognosia
Desires

Repeat back what you've heard without comment, defensiveness or contradiction. We resist reflecting back many important things our patients tell us because:

- *We fear it will make it worse (i.e., delusions, insight, attitudes, medication, etc.)*
- *We do not want to be asked to do something we cannot.*
- *We worry about injuring the therapeutic alliance.*

Delay giving your opinion:

"I promise I will answer your question. If it's alright with you, I would like to first hear more about _____. Okay?"

"I will tell you what I think. I would like to keep listening to your views on this because I am learning a lot I didn't know. Can I tell you later what I think?"

"I will tell you. But I believe your opinion is more important than mine and I would like to learn more before I tell you my opinion. Would that be okay?"

When you finally give your opinion, use the 3 A's:

APOLOGIZE: "I want to apologize because my views might feel hurtful or disappointing."

ACKNOWLEDGE FALLIBILITY: "Also, I could be wrong. I don't know everything."

AGREE: "I hope that we can just agree to disagree. I respect your point of view and I hope you can respect mine."

‖‖‖

LEAP
QUICK START GUIDE

EMPATHIZE

Strategically
express empathy for:

Delusional beliefs
His desire to prove he is not sick
His wish to avoid treatment

Normalize the experience.

AGREE

- Discuss only *perceived* problems/symptoms
- Review advantages and disadvantages of treatment
- Reflect back and highlight the *perceived* benefits

Agree to disagree.

PARTNER

**Move forward on goals you *both* agree
can be worked on together.**

About the Author

Dr. Amador is an internationally sought-after speaker, clinical psychologist, professor at Columbia University, Teachers College, in New York City, the Director of the LEAP Institute and author of eight books.

In 2010, Dr. Amador and his LEAP program are featured in the PBS's NOVA series *This Emotional Life*. Dr. Amador's expertise has made him a regular contributor to the Today Show and a featured guest on ABC's Good Morning America, Prime Time Live, CBS This Morning, NBC Nightly News, 60 Minutes, CNN, Dateline, ABC's World News Tonight, Fox News, The New York Times, The Wall Street Journal, USA Today and many others.

Dr. Amador has been a consultant to numerous companies and government agencies including the National Institute of Health.

His forensic cases include: the Unabomber, PFC Lynndie England, the Elizabeth Smart Kidnapping, and the Zacarias Moussaoui and accused 9/11 co-conspirator Ramsi bin al Shibh trials. Dr. Amador has over 25 years experience working with adults, families, and couples. He lives in New York.

Previously, Dr. Amador was a professor in the Department of Psychiatry at Columbia University, College of Physicians & Surgeons; on the Board of Directors of the National Alliance for the Mentally Ill (NAMI); Director of Research at NAMI; and the Director of Psychology at the New York State Psychiatric Institute.

Dr. Amador has published over 100 peer-reviewed scientific papers, and many other publications that have been translated into more than 20 languages.

Dr. Amador was co-chair of the last text revision of the Schizophrenia and related disorders section of the *DSM IV-TR* (often referred to as the "Psychiatrists' Bible").

LEAP (Listen-Empathize-Agree-Partner) shows clinicians, family members, and law enforcement professionals how to quickly gain the trust of someone who is angry or paranoid. It gives you the tools you need to persuade someone in "denial" about mental illness to accept treatment and/or voluntarily comply with your requests. It grew out of Dr. Xavier Amador's:

- Successful struggle to convince his brother Henry, who was diagnosed with schizophrenia, to take the medications prescribed for him.

- Twenty-five years of hands-on clinical experience with patients who lacked insight.

- Experience gained from hundreds of LEAP seminars involving tons of thousands of clinicians, family members, and law enforcement.

- Twenty-five years of clinical research supported by the NIMH, Stanley Research Foundation, American Psychiatric Association and NARSAD.

Since the book I Am Not Sick, I Don't Need Help! was published, thousands have learned LEAP from the author and LEAP Institute faculty worldwide.

For more information, please visit
www.LEAPInstitute.org